STORIES FROM IRELAND
AND AMERICA

WILLIAM OLIVER O'NEILL

ISBN: 978-1-7328362-4-2

eBook ISBN: 978-1-7328362-5-9

Library of Congress Control Number: 2020939197

Published by Author with assistance from

Bootstrap Books, LLC

Savannah, Georgia

Dedicated to all those mentioned in this book. You are the source of so many happy memories.

Any grammar issues or sentences that go on far too long are intentional. The structures of these stories are in keeping with a rural Irish dialect and are part of my story-telling techniques. I have elected to leave these as is so the voice you hear in these pages is uniquely my own.

CONTENTS

INTRODUCTION

Down through the years I have been encouraged to put my stories into writing. This is my unprofessional attempt to do just that. This is a collection of my stories from my childhood in Ireland and my ministry in America. Some of the stories in this collection may seem to be outlandish or hard to believe! They are all actually true stories.

Life can be compared to a journey. Scenes from the journey, which make a deep impression, remain in the memory. The memory is like a book composed of stories and pictures. The stories and pictures from my journey through life, which are dear to me and have touched me very deeply are of the simple and ordinary events of a gentle and fun-loving people with whom I grew up.

Our early childhood and formative years give us our identity and make us who we become in later life. Our roots go very deep, and no matter where we go, it is always a pleasure to return to the place where we were nurtured. Memories of my childhood are of a simple and uncomplicated upbringing in a rural Irish locality of friendly and hard-working people. They have enabled me to appreciate the beauty of God's creation and the sincerity of the human heart in individuals as they seek out their salvation.

My journey began in 1942. My memory began collecting stories when I was four years of age. I was born at thirty minutes after five on the afternoon of July 21, 1942, at O'Connor's Nursing Home in Tipperary town, Ireland. It is located at the corner of Bridge Street and Abbey Street. Later the building became The Brown Trout Restaurant and it is now a Chinese Restaurant. My father was John O'Neill and my mother was Bridget Kelly. I was born prematurely and was in danger of death, so I was baptized shortly afterwards by Doctor O'Halloran, who delivered me. A week later I was baptized conditionally at St. Michael's Church in Tipperary town. As an infant I was pampered and nursed to good health by my parents, my paternal grandmother, Sarah O'Neill and by my aunt, Maggie O'Neill, who was a spinster sister of my father. Living in the house at this time were my father, mother, grandfather, William, after whom I am named, my grandmother, Sarah, my aunt Maggie, and my unmarried uncles, Willie, Mattie, and Owen. I was the eldest of five children and reared in the family farmhouse, which was built in 1910 on the exact same site as a thatched house, which was demolished to make room for the new house. The farm has been in our family since 1785. My younger brothers were Patrick Joseph, born March 11, 1944, Michael, born October 17, 1945, and Owen Roe, born July 12, 1948. My only sister was Nuala, born December 18, 1958, making her sixteen years younger than me.

My memories of farm life are from the years before Ireland joined the European Union. This was the time of the horse and cart or a donkey and cart. Our mode of transport was a horse, or pony and trap car, or a bicycle. A progressive farmer might have a little Ferguson tractor. Cows were milked out in the field by hand. Later on, the simple milking machine appeared. Most farmers killed their own pigs. Children made a football from the pig's bladder. A hand-pump in the yard was the main source of water. Every farmer grew his own potatoes and cabbage in a little plot called a haggard. The only fertilizer was organic fertilizer. This came from cow and pig manure in a heap of dung neatly piled up near the cow sheds and piggeries. The word cholesterol was unknown. The common diet was plenty of salty bacon, potatoes and cabbage, and homemade bread and butter. Home entertainment was from the wet and dry battery operated radio, when it worked! We walked to school in the morning after milking cows. We walked home from school in the afternoon to milk more cows before attending to home-work by candle light. The Rosary with all "the trimmings" was recited every night.

The rural Ireland in which I lived from 1942 until going to the United States of America in 1967 was very different from the very secular Ireland of today. Friendship and neighborliness were a way of life. Conversation was our national pastime. Church attendance was a priority. *Ní beidh a leithéid ann arís!* Translated from Gaelic means, *it will not be like that again!*

My earliest memory goes back to age of four when one of my morning tasks was to go to my grandfather's bedroom and collect his mug after he had his tea in bed. I can recall visiting my grandfather in hospital before he died. On that occasion he told me that I did not have to collect his mug that day because a nurse had already done this! He died on July 2, 1946, following surgery. I can remember his funeral and the horse drawn hearse, which carried his remains to the cemetery.

Beginning at the age of four my grandmother and my aunt Maggie took me on regular visits to my uncle Pakie in the village of Emly where we stayed for a few days. At this time, my uncle Pakie was not married, and I slept with him in the same single bed. I had to sleep at the foot of the bed with my uncle's toes poking my face. The first time I saw electricity was at my uncle Pakie's house. We did not get electricity in my home until 1949 when I was seven years old.

They say that far away hills are greener. This is very true! The surrounding hills where I grew up seem much greener to me now than they did before I left Ireland for America in 1967. It is not until after we leave what is familiar that we tend to appreciate its beauty. We should never forget who we are and where we come from. Whenever I return to Ireland from city life in America, I am captivated by the majestic beauty of the surrounding countryside. The home where I was reared is surrounded by lovely hills and picturesque villages. These villages are linked together by a maze of narrow roads. Frequently as I lay in bed at night before going to sleep, I travel along those roads in my mind. I recall the names and faces of the families and recall the names of those long dead and buried. Each time I return home there are more new houses and new residents who are unknown to me. Nothing remains constant in this changing world. The cycle of life goes on. So much has changed.

The greatest change is in the method of farming. The physical drudgery is gone. It has been replaced by mental pressure and worry. Smaller farms are being merged together into larger farms. Farming is now a very sophisticated business. There was a time when one raised on a farm could return to it after a long absence and continue with the methods learned as a child, which were passed on from generation to generation. This is no longer the case. The training I received from my father is now obsolete. I was well trained in the ways of farming as it existed then. I have absolutely no idea now as to how to work a farm. The dung-heap has been replaced by the slurry pit. The milk churns have been replaced by the bulk tank. Farm children today would have no idea what a milking stool or spancil looked like. I doubt if they could milk a cow! In fact, the cows of today would not want to be milked by hand!

The following stories from Ireland are typical of the lifestyle of rural Ireland before I left for America in 1967. Life was hard, but it was simple, uncomplicated and wholesome. The people were happy, and they had a great spirit. They were content going about their daily toil. They did what they had to do. They appreciated what they had and managed without what they did not have. While they enjoyed playing pranks on each other, it was harmless and in good fun. They were very loyal to each other and they were great neighbors. They were the salt of the earth. *Ní beidh a leithéid ann arís.* Their likes will not be around again. People are now more sophisticated. Past generations of rural Irish people did not have much formal education, but they were very wise and intelligent. They were gifted with good common sense. This is a quality often lacking in those who have advanced beyond the humble rural schoolhouses of long ago.

With the progress and the convenience of modern technology and the benefits of a more advanced education, we must be careful not to allow the influence and pressure of society to blur our vision of who we really are and where we came from. We must never forget our roots. No matter who or what we are, we are dependent upon the goodness and friendship of each other. We are ultimately dependent upon God and His goodness toward us. Each generation is unique and is a product of its own time and culture. We have received noble values and virtues from past generations. They have given us the warm and happy memories we treasure so much. May future generations have happy childhood memories to share with their children.

PART I
STORIES FROM IRELAND

1

RURAL ELECTRIFICATION

IN 1949, THE RURAL ELECTRIC SCHEME BROUGHT ELECTRICITY to our home. The only rooms in the house electrified were the kitchen, the parlor, my grandmother's bedroom, and an outdoor light. There was also an electric socket for the electric kettle and an electric Sacred Heart lamp. Before getting electricity, we had an oil-burning lamp for light, which was mounted on the wall near the fire. All cooking and bread baking were done over an open fire. AlSo large pots of feeding for farm animals were done over the open fire. One of my tasks as a child was to work the blower to keep the fire going. This was a machine with a large wheel with a belt and handle rotating a small wheel, which had a fan. At night when my mother or aunt sat down by the fire to do some knitting my father who sat opposite read the newspaper while holding it up before the lamp thereby leaving my mother or aunt to work in the dark. The problem was solved by placing another lamp on a nail on the opposite wall. After a year, the entire house, as well as the farmyard houses, were electrified.

2

PRIMARY SCHOOL

WHEN I WAS A PUPIL IN PRIMARY SCHOOL—OR IN THE
National School as it is called in Ireland—I was constantly
reminded by my elders that my school days were the best days
of my life. I did not believe this! I looked upon my primary
school days in the same way as Purgatory. It was a time of
temporary suffering before I could enter the world of adults.
My elders also told me that the teachers had my best interests
at heart. I did not believe this either! I tried not to attract their
attention while in school, and I made every effort to avoid
them outside of school hours. But in later years I came to
appreciate all that my elders had told me. Throughout my adult
life I have maintained contact with every one of my teachers
for as long as they lived. This included my teachers and professors from my other levels of education. It was a very emotional
experience for me several years later when my primary school
teachers knelt before me to receive my blessing as a newly
ordained priest!

All rural pupils walked to and from school. Some had to

walk a distance of two or three miles each way. My home was only a little less than one mile from the school. On the way to school in the mornings we might get a ride on one of the many horse-drawn or donkey-drawn carts taking milk to the creamery, which was very near the school. The chances of getting a ride on the return journey home were slim. We walked in groups and along the way we chatted or got into mischief. We might check the bushes looking for a bird's nest or look for "brickeens" also known as sardines in the river. On my way to school McGrath's cows were grazing along the roadside. During the weeks leading up to the summer holidays we walked barefoot. Until the early 1950s the roads were surfaced with gravel and not paved with tarmacadam. When the weather was wet the roads were very muddy, and in dry weather they were very dusty. It was delightful to feel the soft mud or the dry dust come up between our toes. The negative side of this was getting a toe or the sole of the foot cut when stepping on a small sharp stone. There were very few motorcars on the roads then, and the occasional passing car would leave a trail of thick dust behind it. We had to cover our mouth to avoid inhaling the dust.

In 1947, at the age of five, I started primary school. The school, which was in a rural area, had four rooms. The original two rooms were built in 1876, and the two end rooms were built in 1910. A new school was built in 1952 just up the road from the old school. My father bought the old school and demolished it to use the stones to make a passageway though fields. The school was about one mile from my home, and we walked to and from school. My teacher in the lower grades was Mrs. Bridget O'Donovan, who was an elderly lady with white hair tied in a bun behind her head. As a young teacher, she taught my father some thirty-five to forty years earlier. She insisted that while in her classroom we speak in Gaelic only. In the upper grades my teacher was Mr. Maurice Lacey who was a native of the Gaelic speaking area of Ring, County Waterford. Like Mrs. O'Donovan he, too, insisted that we speak in Gaelic only. The punishment for speaking in English was to stay in after school and write out fifty times in Gaelic, *"Ní beidh mé ag labhairt i mBéarla amárach."* Translated to English, *"I will not be speaking in English tomorrow."* So at a very early age I was introduced to the Gaelic language and I took to it like a duck to water and all through life I have had a deep love and appreciation of our native language.

At the end of my first year in school, my education was interrupted when Dr. Moran, who was our family doctor, decided that my younger brothers, Patrick Joseph and Michael, and I should be confined to bed for one year. This was because my mother had contracted tuberculosis and was placed in a local hospital and later transferred to Peamount Tuberculosis Sanitorium near Dublin. The doctor ordered us confined to bed as a precaution. It was while my mother was in the local hospital in Tipperary town and before being transferred to the sanitorium that my brother Owen Roe was born. Shortly after our confinement to bed, my brothers, Patrick Joseph and Michael, were placed in a children's hospital in Foynes near Limerick city. My paternal grandmother, Sarah O'Neill, and my aunt Maggie, my father's spinster sister, took care of my brother Owen Roe and me at home. My mother was in the sanitorium for two years. I never saw her during this time. When she returned home after two years, I was eight years old and because I had not seen here since the age of six, I had forgotten what she looked like, but I did remember her distinctive striped overcoat. When she arrived home, she was wearing that overcoat and that was how I recognized her.

During the time of my one-year absence from school and confinement to bed, my grandmother and my aunt assumed the role of teachers and each day they spent time with me doing reading, writing, and arithmetic, as well as intense instruction in the catechism of the Catholic Church and learning my prayers. So I can say I was "homeschooled" during this time. This turned out to be a great blessing for me when I returned to school after an absence of one year. Upon my return to school my teacher, Mrs. O'Donovan, placed me in a lower grade instead of advancing me to join my previous classmates. Then I got a lucky break a few days later when during a reading and questioning and answering session she discovered that my knowledge was very advanced, and she immediately promoted me to a higher grade to join my previous classmates.

I remained at the local primary or national school until September of 1954 after I had just moved into fifth grade, which was two years prior to completing primary school level of education. In Ireland, primary school level ends with sixth grade. At that time my parents transferred me to the Christian Brothers' Primary School in Tipperary town, which was a distance of six miles from my home. The reason for transferring me to the Christian Brothers' Primary School to complete my primary education was to give a better education before I would stay home and take up farming. The Christian Brothers had a reputation for giving an excellent primary education superior to that at the local rural primary school. I was the eldest son, and so it was expected that I would become a farmer on the family farm. In those days, post-primary education was not seen as necessary to become a farmer. During my two years as a pupil at the Christian Brothers' Primary School in Tipperary, I cycled the twelve miles return journey each day regardless of the weather. I must confess that on one occasion when it was pouring rain, I deliberately stood under a drain spout and got myself soaking wet so that I would not have to go to school in soaking wet clothes. When I was good and soaked, I cycled home. But my father made me change my clothes and put me and my bicycle into the van and drove me into school. In a stern voice, he told me that I had a choice of either going to school to finish my primary education or just forget about it and stay home and begin farming immediately. It was very tempting for me to decide on staying at home and begin farming, but at that point I had discovered the wonderful world of primary school girls, who were also cycling their bikes to the Convent of Mercy Primary School, a girls only school, which was directly across the street from the Christian Brothers' Primary School, a boys only school. While I was interested in being a farmer, I needed more time to play!

3

FIRST CONFESSION AND HOLY COMMUNION

BECAUSE I WAS ABSENT FROM SCHOOL WHEN MY CLASSMATES were making their First Holy Communion, I received it shortly after returning to school. But before doing this I had to meet for four consecutive Saturdays with the local priest, Father Michael B. O'Dwyer, at his house in Cappwahite. Father O'Dwyer was a very big man with a very stern look. I was terrified of him. During each session he asked me several questions and had me recite prayers from memory. Having been well instructed in the catechism during the time of my confinement to bed, I had no problem passing the test. He informed my aunt that I should come to his house on the following Saturday before morning Mass to make my First Confession and make my First Holy Communion at the Mass that morning. I will never understand why he did not arrange for my first confession at the church in the confession box. So my First Confession was face-to-face kneeling on the floor before the stern face Father O'Dwyer sitting in his chair in his living room.

On the way to Father O'Dwyer's house to make my First

Confession, I was seated behind my aunt on the carrier of her bicycle. As she was cycling up Connery's steep hill, I asked her what I should tell the priest in confession. While she was giving me a list of my sins, I kept pushing my feet against the tire of the rear wheel of her bicycle thereby making it very difficult for her to peddle up the steep hill. Unfortunately for me, she looked down and saw my feet pushing against the tire of the wheel and realized why she was having difficulty cycling up the hill. She immediately got down from her bike and gave a severe slap across my face and told me to tell Father O'Dwyer that I was a bold brat.

4

MY NEW BICYCLE

SHORTLY AFTER THIS MY AUNT PRESENTED ME WITH A GIFT OF a lovely red bicycle. It was a small bike for a child and had a most unusual shape. It had a stand attached for parking. This was indeed a most unusual feature for a bike at that time. She taught me how to ride it. I was the only child in the locality who had my own personal bike and I was the envy of all. Oh, how I loved to show off with it. But my showing off brought me embarrassment one day. I was peddling on the bike while it was in the parked position on the stand and while facing a wall the bike dropped from the parking stand and the bike and myself crashed into the wall. Now I was a laughing stock, and to add insult to injury my aunt impounded the bike for a week and made me walk.

5

MY CONFIRMATION

ON MAY 11, 1954, I RECEIVED CONFIRMATION IN Cappawhite Church. That day was also a Fair Day or Market Day in the village. My father purchased two cows that day. I had a brand new suit of clothes and new shoes for the occasion. In those days most boys of my age wore short pants. I tried to convince my parents to let me have long pants for confirmation, but my father insisted that I get short pants because I was not tall enough for long pants. After the Confirmation ceremony my father put a cane in my hand and made me walk the two cows to my home three miles away.

6

WINNIE MCGRATH'S HOUSE

WHILE WALKING HOME FROM SCHOOL ONE AFTERNOON I GOT myself into big trouble. Passing Winnie McGrath's house with a group of boys and girls, Winnie McGrath was standing at her door. The front wall and door of her house was close to the side of the road. The river flowed parallel to the other side of the road. Some of us got into a bit of mischief in the river. Winnie McGrath reprimanded us and told us to go on home. I picked up a fistful of wet soggy clay and threw it at the lovely yellow-ochre painted wall of her house. Then we all took off running, and I could hear Winnie McGrath shouting that she would tell my father about this.

When my father heard about it later that afternoon, he gave me a good whacking. Then he got on his bicycle and told me to run ahead of him down to Winnie McGrath to offer an apology. He cycled behind me and made me run ahead of him at great speed. When we arrived at Winnie McGrath's house, I made my apology, and then my father ordered me to wash the clay from the wall. When I had done this, my father gave me another whacking and made me offer another apology to Winnie McGrath.

Several years later when I was ordained a priest, I called on Winnie McGrath to give her my blessing. When she got down on her knees outside her door just underneath the spot where my fistful of clay had soiled her lovely yellow-ochre wall, she smiled and asked me if I remembered that incident. I told her that I would never forget it. Then I gave her my blessing, and she kissed the hand that threw the fistful of clay at her wall. Until recently that house still had its thatched roof and yellow-ochre walls and whenever I pass it, I recall that day of long ago and the punishment I received from my father for being a bad boy.

7

SCHOOL EXCURSIONS

DURING THE SUMMER HOLIDAYS, OUR TEACHER, MR. MAURICE Lacey, took us on an excursion to the seaside. However, the first excursion was after the summer holidays in September 1950 when I was eight years old. It consisted of a very small group of ten pupils. The excursion was to Youghal in County Cork. Mr. Lacey took his wife and daughter and two pupils in his black Ford Prefect car, registration number HI 6636. The other eight pupils, including me, traveled in a station wagon owned by a taxi driver called Mr. Johnny Davis from Tipperary town. It was on that excursion to the seaside in Youghal that I saw the sea for the first time. Coming home that night in the dark we saw little bright spots reflecting in the headlights along the middle of the road. Our driver, Mr. Johnny Davis, informed us that they were cat's eyes! When we returned to school after that excursion, we were very excited telling the other pupils about our great adventure in a faraway place and all the things we saw, which we had never seen before, such as the ocean and rolling waves and tide and the cat's eyes along the middle of the road. We felt like world travelers!

After the first school excursion in 1950, word of its exciting adventure spread and arrangements were made to hire a bus for the following summer for an excursion on a larger scale. Parents would also be welcome to travel. School excursions to the seaside became an annual event during the summer holiday. A bus was provided by Mr. T. K. O'Donoghue from Tipperary town. To make paying the cost easier, those who intended to travel were asked to sign up and contribute one penny per week during the course of the year. Our teacher, Mr. Lacy, kept a special notebook in which he recorded our weekly contributions. When making the penny contribution to the teacher, we said in Gaelic, *"Pingin I dtreó an turas."* Translated to English is, *"A penny toward the excursion."* When school closed for the summer holidays our excursion fare was usually paid in full. If we had overpaid, we got the excess back for spending money.

On the morning of the excursion, we waited near the creamery for the arrival of the bus. The day at the seaside was spent walking on the strand, going to the carnival grounds, and taking a swim. To take a swim, we rented swimming gear and changed clothes in little box-stalls located on the strand. Coming out from the stalls other pupils would cheer and make uncomplimentary comments about how one looked in swimming gear. We returned home very late at night after a wonderful day at the seaside. When school reopened in September, we started all over again collecting our pennies for the following year's excursion.

8
_____

THE SCHOOL DENTIST

Once a year under the Irish National Health Scheme, a dentist came to the school to check our teeth. I remember having a tooth extracted in school. It was my first encounter with a dentist. I was absolutely terrified going into him because those who had gone in before me to the classroom where the torture was taking place were screaming while they were with him. When they came out, they were spitting out blood and obviously in great pain. The older children were telling the younger ones that the dentist would take out our tongues if they did not look good. As I sat on a chair, which was the teacher's desk chair, the sight of the big needle and the pliers in the hands of the dentist was terrifying. He told me there was a bad one in there and he was going to pull it out. I screamed while he was taking it out. When he had removed the tooth, he tossed it into a bucket, which was near the chair. Inside the bucket were lots of teeth and bloody pieces of cotton wool. There was blood everywhere. Pupils who had teeth extracted were looking into each other's mouths comparing their wounds. That annual visit from the school dentist was dreaded. After that I got wise and played sick and stayed home on that day for the remainder of my time in primary school.

9
___

FIRE IN THE SCHOOL

WE BROUGHT OUR OWN LUNCH TO SCHOOL. THIS WAS A FEW slices of bread and butter and a bottle of milk. We placed our bottle of milk on the window ledge in the classroom after removing the cork from the bottle. Sometimes the corks were made from rolled up paper. School lunches brings to mind an event which got me into serious trouble and could have been a great disaster for the school. During lunch period on one particular day, our teacher, Mrs. O'Donovan, had gone to her residence at the rear of the school for her own lunch. A few of us decided to toast our bread over the fire in the classroom fireplace. We placed our slices of bread on two little sticks and held them over a very poor lighted fire. Adjoining the classroom, was an unused classroom with plenty of empty cardboard boxes. The windows in that room were broken and boarded up. Because of the very poor lighted fire in Mrs. O'Donovan's classroom, I got the bright idea of bringing out some pieces of cardboard and papers to place in the fire in order to get it burning good and well so that we could toast our bread. Because the fire

9

in the fireplace was almost extinguished the cardboard, which was damp would not light up, but only smolder. So I took the smoldering cardboard back to the adjoining disused classroom and pushed it out into the school yard through the boards in the boarded up window and returned to the fireplace to try another way to get the fire going.

Shortly after this, someone shouted that the adjoining unused classroom was on fire! This was because after I pushed the smoldering cardboard out through the boarded up window, it landed on one of the girls sitting outside the window. She pushed it back in through the same opening, and it came to rest on the window ledge inside where there were stacks of papers, which caught fire. By now a big fire was raging in the unused classroom, and at this time Mrs. O'Donovan returned from her lunch. She tried to beat out the fire with a stick and had the pupils throw cans of water on it. The fire was eventually put out, but the boards on the boarded up window were badly burned.

Mrs. O'Donovan then carried out an investigation into the cause of the fire. Several voices in unison loudly said, "Willie Oliver O'Neill was playing with a burning piece of cardboard." The truth of the matter was that it was the girl outside the window who pushed the burning cardboard back in who caused the fire! I got a very severe punishment from Mrs. O'Donovan, and when she was finished with me, she had the other teacher, Mr. Lacy, do another round of punishment on me.

THE SCHOOL WELL

OUT IN A FIELD NEAR THE SCHOOL, WAS A SHALLOW OPEN well, which had lovely clear crystal drinking water. Pupils had to take turns to stay in after school hours to sweep the classroom floors. Water was sprinkled on the floors to keep down the dust. The pupils assigned to sweep the rooms would bring water from the well in old paint cans.

During playtime some pupils would go to the well for a drink of the crystal clear cold water. On one occasion when several boys and girls were flat on their stomachs lapping up water with their hands, a boy who I will not name, but not me, stood up and urinated into the well. This caused the pupils who were drinking the water to get angry and get upset stomachs. Eventually the news of this disgusting act of pollution reached our teacher, Mrs. O'Donovan. Her family lived in the teacher's residence next to the school and used the water from the well for their domestic purposes. The boy who polluted the well was severely punished by Mrs. O'Donovan. It was to be a long time again before we drank crystal clear cold water from the school well.

11

PEEPHOLE IN THE SCHOOL TOILET

IN 1952, THE OLD LOCAL PRIMARY SCHOOL WAS REPLACED BY a new school. The separate toilets for the boys and girls were outside in their playgrounds. They were very primitive. Because the boys frequently invaded the girl's playground and because he toilet door did not have a latch or lock, when a girl was using it, there was always another girl guarding it on the outside.

In 1952, when we relocated to the new school, the toilets there were considered state of the art. The new toilets were located in one building at the rear of the school. A fence separated the entrance to the boy's and girl's toilets. Inside the building, both toilets were separated by a single-layer concrete block wall. Boys were curious to know what was going on at the girl's side of the wall. Two boys solved the problem by removing a concrete block. This took several days to accomplish. They had a hammer and chisel. Each day they chipped away at the concrete block. Boys, who noticed this operation, were warned to keep this to themselves; otherwise, they would suffer torturous consequences. After a few days, the concrete block was successfully removed from the base of the wall, and the girls did not notice it.

The boys were now lining up for a peep into the girl's toilet. Because there was such a demand for a peep, the two boys, who had removed the concrete block, saw a financial opportunity. They charged a halfpenny for a peep, or three peeps for one penny. Most pupils did not have any money. Desperation leads to a solution. Boys were asking their parents that night for money to purchase pencils or notebooks. Some boys were unable to get the money.

The next day, those who had money got in line for as many peeps as they could afford. Meanwhile, the girls were unaware of all the peeping. The show came to an abrupt end when one boy, who could not afford a peep, put his hand through the peephole. This gave the girls a fright, and they ran screaming to the teachers to report the invasion of their privacy. Both teachers, a man and a woman, came out to investigate. The man investigated from the boy's toilet, and the woman investigated from the girl's toilet. All the boys were summoned to the male teacher's classroom. He was raging and wanted those boys, who had removed the concrete block, to confess. The two culprits sat at their desks looking very innocent. When the other boys looked in their direction, they got angry looks in return. When nobody was confessing, the teacher then threatened to have the police come and interrogate. There was still no admission by the two boys. The other boys were not going to betray them. This was partly because of a sense of loyalty and probably more because of fear that they would be tortured by the two boys if they informed the teacher. In spite of all his threats, the teacher failed to find out who removed the concrete block.

Next day, the teacher had the building contractor on site to replace the missing concrete block. As well as that, he ordered another layer of concrete blocks to be built on both sides of the single-layer concrete block wall. Now the wall dividing the girl's and boy's toilets had three layers of concrete blocks, instead of one layer. That was the end of the toilet peephole. The two boys never let it be known how much money they collected from the peeps. Life moved on from there, and the teachers never found out who removed the concrete block.

12

THE MOUSE IN THE SCHOOL

ONE EVENING, I CAPTURED A MOUSE IN THE HAY BARN AND put it into a little box. Next day, I put the box with the mouse in it into my school bag and took it to school. During class period when I thought it as the right moment, I let the mouse out of the box. It scurried across the floor and the girls were screaming and our teacher, Mrs. O'Donovan, put her knees together and held her long skirt against her legs to make sure that mouse did not run up inside her skirt. The mouse eventually escaped out under the door. Unfortunately, earlier in the day I had shown the mouse in the box to a few others, so I was immediately charged with letting the mouse loose in the classroom. I received the usual punishment as well as staying in after school to write out fifty times that I would never again bring a mouse to school.

26

13

SECONDARY SCHOOL

After I completed Primary School in 1956 at age 14, I wanted to continue at the Christian Brothers Secondary School. But my parents decided that if I wanted to stay in school instead of remaining at home on the farm, I should be locked up in a boarding school where I could give full attention to my studies. I did not like this, but I was not ready yet to take up farming.

My parents checked on the cost of a number of boarding schools. The least expensive one they found was St. Peter's College in Wexford located in the South East of Ireland. It was just over one hundred miles from my home. The decision was made to send me there. To prepare for this I had to get new clothes, and this time I was allowed to get long pants! In September 1956, my father and his cousin, Simon O'Neill, drove me to Wexford in Simon O'Neill's Hillman Minx car, registration number AHI 542. They were seated in the front of the car, and I was in the rear seat feeling like a bad boy being sent away to a reformatory school!

Residing in a boarding school was a major adjustment. It was my first time away from home for an extended period. It took some time to get to know a few hundred boys by name, especially the ones who were senior to me. It took some time to adjust to such things as eating meals in a refectory with several hundred boys, sleeping in a dormitory with several hundred beds, sitting at a desk for several hours of study every evening in a large study hall, and having to attend daily religious services in the chapel.

The first time I entered the refectory and chapel I was amazed to see about one hundred priests, or who I later found out were not priests, even though they were dressed like priests. They were actually seminarians, who were students preparing for the priesthood. There was a seminary or training college for priests attached to the secondary school. The seminarians shared the same refectory and chapel with the secondary school students. After I graduated from secondary school five years later, I decided to study for the priesthood and became a seminarian there at St. Peter's in Wexford.

Most of the students were from County Wexford. They had weekend visits from their family. Being so far away from home, I did not see my family until holiday time. I was constantly looking forward to letters from home with all the news. I was very homesick. There were times I was tempted to run away, but where could I run to? Running home was out of the question! As time went on, I adjusted and remained there until graduation some five years later in 1961. During that time, I formed many friendships, which have lasted ever since.

14

GROWING UP ON THE FARM

MY FATHER WAS A DAIRY FARMER. HE TAUGHT ME TO MILK cows when I was eight years old. As soon as I was considered to have mastered the art of milking cows, I had to milk three cows each morning and again the evening. Until we got a milking machine some years later, we had a few people hired to help with the milking. They sang songs while milking. Cows were then milked out in the field. My father delayed getting a milking machine because he believed it was an unnatural way to milk a cow. Eventually he had to get one because it became difficult to find people to do the milking. During the long summer holidays from school, I had to work on the farm. Periodically there was an electric failure, which meant the milking machine would not work and all cows had to be milked by hand. Since we no longer had hired help for milking, this meant all of the family had to milk all of the cows by hand. This could be anywhere between eight or ten cows each. This was very tiring on one's wrists. Because I was the eldest my father had taught me from a very young age how to reap and sow, to plough and mow, and to be a farmer's boy. This was all done by horses. But I was also fortunate to have access to working with tractors and gain a good knowledge of the maintenance of farm machinery. I learned much of this from my uncle Mattie, who lived with us and who was an agricultural contractor. As such, he had a lot of machinery, which included a tractor, a threshing machine, a reaper and binder, a plough, a mowing machine, and a drain digger. He taught me about the basic internal workings of tractor engines and the internal mechanism of a threshing machine. To this day, I am fascinated with machinery, and I try to keep up with the latest farming technology.

As a farm child, I was seen as extra help for work outside of school hours. There was milk to be taken to the creamery on a horse and cart, milk churns to be washed after returning from the creamery, pigs and calves to be fed, piggeries to be cleaned out, potatoes to be dug out of the ground each day for dinner, hedges to be trimmed, weeds and thistles to be cut in the fields, drains to be cleaned, and cows to be milked by hand before we got a milking machine in 1958. There was an unending list of other tasks. By mid-July hay saving was in full swing. The days were spent in the meadows from early morning until milking time in the evening. The hay was cut by a mowing machine drawn by a pair of horses or by a tractor. In warm weather, the horses needed plenty of water to drink. This meant walking across fields from the pump in the farmyard, hauling heavy buckets of water to the horses in the meadow. This was back-breaking work especially for a child. After the hay was cut, it was dried out and made into little stacks. A few days later, the stacks were trimmed and secured with ropes made from hay called sugáns to withstand any rain or wind. It was important that one of the sugáns on the haystack faced toward the west or as we used to say toward the Limerick wind. This was a monotonous and tedious job going from one stack of hay to another.

The best memories I have of saving hay are drinking tea in the meadow. The meadow or hayfield was a place that always gave one a great appetite. Eyes were constantly looking in the direction of the farmyard waiting for the arrival of the bucket of tea and the black currant soda bread laced with butter and jam. A mug of tea had a delightful flavor in the meadow sitting under a stack of hay, or in a grassy area under a bush, or in the shade from the sun. When all the hay was saved, the stacks were brought into the hay barn on a float. It was a great delight for a child to get a ride on a hay float. Farmers did not mind children riding on a hay float when it was empty, but it could be an annoyance to them when there was a stack of hay on it because the children would climb up on the back of the float behind the stack of hay and cause the loose hay to fall off.

During the summer holidays from school we were sent on holidays to the house of a cousin or relative. They were not actually holidays in the proper sense of the word. They could be called working holidays! Going on the so called holidays to a cousin or relative meant helping them on their farm by doing the same work we were doing at home. Then the cousins or relatives returned the compliment by sending their children to our farm to help us. But because it was an opportunity for us to be somewhere other than home, we saw this exchange of child labor as being holidays!

PLOUGHING FOR POTATOES

ALONG WITH DAIRY FARMING MY FATHER GREW SEVERAL acres of potatoes, which he sold on Saturdays at the Market Yard in Tipperary town. He was an excellent ploughman and took great pride in ploughing a straight furrow with a plough pulled by two horses. Opening the first furrow in a green field was the key. On one occasion when opening the first furrow in a new field he had me go to the other end and stand there as a marker. He set out with an eye ahead to where I was standing. But mischief got the better of me, and I foolishly decided to test his skill. I kept moving very gradually to one side. After moving a few feet, I could see that the furrow was curving and was no longer a straight line. So I gradually moved back to my original position, which then caused the furrow to curve in the other direction. When my father arrived at the end of the field with his horses and plough, he looked back and saw a very crooked furrow. This upset him very much and he took a wrench from the plough and ran toward me and I took off running as fast as I could. I climbed over a fence of blackthorn bushes and escaped in to the next field. But more trouble awaited me there. There was an agitated bull in the field, and he came running toward me. I was very frightened and climbed back again into the field I had escaped from. I ran into the arms of my father, who had been watching the danger I had been in. My father was so relieved that I escaped from the bull that he was no longer upset over my causing him to plough a crooked furrow. However, he made me turn back the crooked upturned sod, and when that was done, he set out again to start a new furrow while I stood still at the other end as a marker.

16

THE POTATO MARKET

EACH SATURDAY MORNING IN THE WINTER MONTHS WHILE IT was still dark, my father and I left home with a horse and cart-load of potatoes in six-stone sacks for the market yard, in Tipperary town, a distance of six miles. For those not familiar with weight in stones, one stone equals fourteen pounds. So a six-stone sack of potatoes weighs eighty-four pounds. On arrival at the market yard my father unloaded the sacks of potatoes and returned home the six-mile journey for a second load, leaving me to stay with the sacks of potatoes. Upon his return with the second load, the customers were arriving. Other farmers were also there selling their potatoes. Dad had his regular customers who came to the Market Yard. He also had customers in private homes and fish and chip shops, and it was my task to walk to all those customers to take their orders, which I wrote down. When I returned from my rounds, these orders were set aside, and the surplus amount of potatoes were sold to the customers in the market yard. Customers ordered varied amounts, which were weighed on a scale by a lady called

Miss Falbey, who I remember as being very refined and gracious. When she arrived in the market yard before the customers and before my father returned with the second load of potatoes, Miss Falbey greeted me and praised me for being a good little boy to stay in the market yard on my own in the early morning darkness protecting the sacks of potatoes. I took advantage of her generosity by telling her I was starving with hunger after being there since an early hour. She always had a bar of chocolate ready for me because she knew I would let her know that I was hungry. After the customers had all left by late morning, my father and I made deliveries with the reserved orders to private homes and fish and chip shops. He had a man from the town helping him with the deliveries. The man's name was "Skinny" Egan. I never knew the man's first name! After all deliveries were completed, my father took me to a restaurant, or what he called "an eating house." After our meal, which was very late in the afternoon and getting close to darkness, we set out for the six-mile journey home with a very tired horse, who was now making his fourth six mile walk in one day. In other words, the poor old horse was making the second twelve-mile return trip the same day, a total of twenty-four miles.

17

MY FATHER'S DRIVING LESSONS

ONE SATURDAY EVENING IN 1952 ON OUR RETURN HOME FROM
the potato market on the horse and cart when I was ten years
old, my father told me that making twelve mile return journey
twice each Saturday by horse and cart was a very slow way to be
traveling, and that he was going to purchase a van and learn to
drive it. He was then 48 years of age. After our meal on the
following Saturday he went to Evans Garage in Tipperary town
and purchased a second-hand 5 cwt blue Ford van, registration
number IU 5154. Part of the deal was that the garage owner
would provide driving instructions for as long as it took for my
father to learn to drive alone.

My father took daily driving lessons from Connie Dundon
who was an employee of Evans Garage in Tipperary. Very few
people in the locality were able to drive a car at that time.
When my father got behind the wheel for his first lesson, he
took off his hat and blessed himself. In this first lesson the plan
was that Connie Dundon would explain the functions of the
clutch, brake, and accelerator, and he would change the gears

while my father operated the clutch as instructed. As they prepared for take-off, my father kept letting the clutch out too fast while he had the accelerator all the way to the floorboard. This caused the van to jump forward and stall the engine. Finally they got going and went along for a mile or so until they came to a main road where he had to stop. Connie told my father to take his foot of the accelerator and gently push the brake. But Dad pushed the brake so hard that the van came to a sudden stop and all of us in the rear went forward into the laps of Connie Dundon and my father.

During this time while learning to drive, he went through the driving motions every night by the kitchen fire. He sat on a chair with three sods of turf on the floor and the fire thongs stuck into a bucket of turf. The three sods of turf on the floor represented the clutch, brake, and accelerator. The thongs in the bucket of turf represented the gear lever. In front of him was an imaginary ignition key, choker, and starter. He went through the motions beginning with turning on the ignition key, pulling out the choker, and then the starter. He made humming sounds representing the sounds of the engine running. Then he put his left foot on the sod of turf representing the clutch and moved the thongs into first gear, then taking his foot off the sod of turf and putting his right foot on the sod of turf representing the accelerator. He repeated the process for each gear movement. When it was time to stop, he placed his left foot on the sod of turf representing the clutch and his right foot on the sod of turf representing the brake. In this simple way, he practiced his driving each night by the fireside.

This van had only three forward gears and the reverse. The gear movements were in the shape of the letter "H," which

Connie Dundon drew on the dashboard. Around this time, a neighbor, Jim Breen was also learning to drive. He had a Morris Minor car, which had four forward gears. One evening Jim Breen and my father were discussing gear movements. Of course, both of them thought that their respective vehicles had the same number of forward gears. My father not knowing that Jim Breen's car had four forward gears, and Jim Breen not knowing that my father's van had only three forward gears, the two of them got into an argument over the correct gear movements. Jim Breen tried to explain to my father that his car had four forward gears, and my father insisted that there was no such thing as a car having four forward gears. Jim Breen then upset my father by telling him that he had an inferior vehicle, which was lacking an extra gear. My father said that he did not need four gears, because two forward gears were plenty for him! He did not even need the third hear.

18

THE PONY AND TRAP CAR

PRIOR TO MY FATHER LEARNING TO DRIVE, WE WENT TO Sunday Mass and to shopping in Tipperary town on a pony and trap car. The pony's name was Mossy, who was then over 20 years of age, and had been in the family since he was a baby foal. The trap car was a box-like cart with seating for three facing each other sideways. There was a door at one end with an outside step, which was used to enter the trap car. Some trap cars were designed differently having back-to-back seats, and others had the seats facing outward over the wheels like the ones seen on the movie "The Quiet Man." On cold days, we had a blanket on our laps. When it rained, an oilcloth was placed over the blanket. This could be tricky because the cloth could fill up with water if it was slackened, and the weight of the water could cause it to collapse thereby drenching the occupants. At a certain time of the year when the pony was shedding hair, we had to cover our clothes with old overcoats. On arrival at our destination, the cushions were removed from the seats and placed inside in case of rain. The pony was fed with a bag of oats placed under his mouth and suspended from a rope around the top of his neck.

My father and a next-door neighbor, Tom O'Neill, took an annual holiday in Lisdoonvarna where sulfur springs and wells were plentiful. They went there to avail of the mineral waters, which were reputed to relieve pains. They travelled to Lisdoon-varna by bus. But when my father learned to drive, he drove there in his van. Because he was away on a weekend, we had to take the pony and trap car to Sunday Mass. The pony was now old and retired and was not happy about being reactivated. When we went to catch him in the field, he ran in circles around us. When we finally caught him, I was annoyed with him and I made the bad mistake of standing behind him while giving him a slap on his rear end with a stick. He raised his back legs and kicked me under the chin and broke my jawbone. I have a mark under my chin to this day, which is given as an identification for my body should it ever be needed!

19

CONNIE RYAN

AS WELL AS GROWING POTATOES FOR SALE AND DAIRY
farming, my father raised a large number of young pigs, or
piglets, which were called bonhams. Whenever I think of all
the sows and bonhams we had at home in Ballykiveen, the
name of one particular man always comes to mind. That man
was Connie Ryan. He was what could be called an unqualified
veterinary surgeon. Whenever an animal was sick the local
farmers would first seek the opinion of Connie Ryan. He was
very knowledgeable in making a diagnosis on a sick animal.
Upon arrival, he carefully checked the sick animal. He did this
without speaking a word while the onlookers waited for his
verdict. After he completed his investigation and before
uttering a word, he put his hand in his pocket and took out his
pipe and tobacco. In silence, he went through the ritual of
cutting the tobacco, then filling his pipe, lighting it, and taking
a deep puff before putting the lid on the pipe. After a few puffs,
he took another look at the animal. Instead of giving a verdict
there and then, he told about a similar case he saw sometime in

the past. Then he went into a lengthy monologue on the details of that case he was recalling. During all this time, one did not dare interrupt Connie by asking him to give his opinion on the cow he was now examining. Should you interrupt him, he sternly reprimanded you and asked you to wait and let him finish his story to see why he was coming to a definite conclusion on what was making the animal sick. If he was not sure of his diagnosis, he would admit it and suggest getting a qualified veterinary surgeon. But usually Connie Ryan was able to make an accurate diagnosis. He would prescribe a medication such as a good dose of salts or a tin of treacle. On one particular occasion, he prescribed a most unusual medication for a young bull we had who injured his penis when he tried to jump over a gate. The injury was so severe that the bull's penis swelled up like a balloon. Connie Ryan said that the best cure for such an injury was to massage it a few times a day with stale urine, which we should collect in a bucket. My poor father almost puked up his guts! We were amused by this cure. But our amusement ended when Connie Ryan stated that the urine should be so stale that we would be unable to tolerate the smell of it. This was too much for my father, and so he immediately rejected Connie Ryan's remedy and decided to send for the veterinary surgeon to attend to the misfortunate bull.

Connie Ryan walked everywhere. He never learned to ride a bicycle. His work took him all over the locality and far beyond it. Because we did not have telephones then, when Connie was needed a child was usually sent on a bicycle to summon him and Connie would follow on foot. In cases of emergency, he was collected by the farmer who needed his assistance. He always made regular calls to check on sick animals he had previously examined. His main occupation was thatching houses and killing pigs and castrating young bonhams. I don't think he received any payment for his consultation services. His usual reward was to be invited into the farmhouse for a few bottles of Guinness, or porter as it was called. While he consumed his beer sitting by the fireside in the kitchen, he smoked his pipe and told stories from the distant past about some unusual animal illnesses that he treated.

20

BUYING SOWS AND BONHAMS

SOMETIMES WE HAD AS MANY AS TEN OR TWELVE SOWS AT home. My father bought them to markets or in response to advertisements in the local weekly papers "The Nationalist" or "The Limerick Leader." But most of the time he bought them from a man by the name of Philly Ryan, locally known as Philly Whip of Ballinvassa near the village of Donohill. Philly made his living buying and selling sows and bonhams here and there and selling them to local farmers. He travelled the countryside in a covered green Volkswagen pick-up truck with a sow and a litter of bonhams. He did not drive, but his son also named Philly did the driving. At regular intervals, he arrived at our farmyard with a sow and a litter of bonhams trying to make a sale with my father. He would say to my father, "Johnny, I have a grand sow with a lovely litter of bonhams here for you. I know you will not let me leave the yard without taking them." My father's response was, "For God's sake go away Philly, 'tis too many of them I have, and lately there is no profit in pigs." The Philly usually replied, "Johnny just take a look at them." My father would go over to the truck and pretend to take a disinterested look and say, "God bless them, they are grand, but what the use, I have enough for now." Then Philly would say, "Johnny, take them and they will be a very lucky litter, and you being such a good customer, I will let you have them for a price you can't refuse." Between the hopping and the trotting and the bantering and bargaining, my father usually bought the lovely litter of bonhams. When the price was agreed as well as the amount of money to be returned to my father for "good luck," the deal was sealed with Philly Whip as customary, spitting on the palm of his right hand and my father receiving a slap from him on the open palm of his right hand.

21

___

SOWS FARROWING

ABOUT EVERY WEEK WE HAD A SOW FARROWING THEREBY
adding an extra litter of bonhams. Every house and shed we had
was full of bonhams. It was easy to tell in advance when a sow
was getting close to delivering a litter of bonhams. Before the
introduction of farrowing pens, the children in the family were
given the task of keeping an eye on the very pregnant sow. If
the sow was unattended during and after delivering, there was a
danger that the bonhams might get trapped underneath her
when she lay down. When it was obvious that a sow was going
to deliver during the night, someone had to stay up all night and
keep watch and stay up for a few nights after the birth until the
bonhams were strong and lively enough to get out of the way of
the sow as she lay down. With the introduction of farrowing
pens, staying up for a few nights was no longer necessary. The
farrowing pen was designed in such way that when the sow laid
down slowly her young had time to avoid being trapped under
her. The sow was in the narrow center part of the pen while the
bonhams were in spacious pockets to the side at a slightly lower

level. When the sow began to lay down slowly, the bonhams had plenty of time to get back into lower level spacious pockets and avoid being trapped or hurt.

Prior to giving birth the sow got very sick and spent some time making a bed of straw for herself. When it was time to deliver her litter, she lay down on the straw and stretched out on her side. When the first bonham arrived, the others arrived one by one at regular intervals. As soon as each bonham made its entry into the world, the person attending took it in his hand and cut the umbilical cord with a scissors and then removed a spongy substance from its mouth and wiped the little new-born with straw or hay. Then it was taken into the kitchen and placed in a box near the fire to keep it warm. This procedure followed with each bonham until it was estimated that most of the littler had arrived. At this time, the bonhams in the box by the fire were brought out one by one and placed beside the mother sow and given a nipple to get their first suckle of milk. The particular nipple given to the bonham for its first suckle from that moment onward became that bonham's nipple for suckling. When bringing the bonham to the sow from the box by the fire, it was very important to keep the bonham from squealing. A squealing bonham would upset the mother sow. Doing this, the trick was to hold the bonham by one of its ears. I have no idea why this method worked, but it never failed. After the entire litter of bonhams were brought to the mother sow, she started making a distinctive continuous grunt called "warping," which meant she was allowing her milk to flow from her nipples. Watching the entire litter suckling was a sight to behold. My father looked on very contentedly saying, "God bless them."

22

CLIPPING A BONHAM'S TEETH

BONHAMS ARE BORN WITH VERY SHARP SMALL TEETH. WHEN suckling from the mother's nipples, their sharp teeth pinched her nipples. For this reason, it was necessary to clip their teeth with a small sharp clipper shortly after birth. This may seem cruel, but it was not. Their teeth were like needles and very brittle. After the baby teeth were clipped, all that remained were the roots. New teeth grew, which were stronger and thicker and did not pinch the sow's nipples.

When clipping the baby teeth, one person sat on a chair and held the bonham lying on its back while holding all four legs together. Another person used the clippers to clip the teeth. Their teeth were so brittle that they broke off easily. Each bonham was marked on its back with shoe polish following the dental surgery. This identified the ones whose teeth were clipped. During the surgery, the person holding the bonham while sitting on a chair was likely to receive a squirt of urine. Because the bonham was laying on its back in the person's lap, a female bonham would simply wet the person, but if it was a male bonham, and one was not alert, it was possible to get a squirt of urine in the face!

23

CASTRATING BONHAMS

A FEW WEEKS AFTER THEIR BIRTH, THE MALE BONHAMS WERE castrated if they were not intended for breeding purposes. My father did not rear any young pigs for breeding. All our pigs were for sale at the pig market when they were a few months old. Castrated pigs grew and thrived faster. Castrating young pigs was a very delicate procedure, which required the services of Connie Ryan. He arrived on foot at the arranged date and time and on entering the pig house usually said to my father, "That's a fine litter you have here, Johnny, God bless them."

The way in which the young pigs were handled for this surgical procedure was something similar to the way they were handled for clipping their teeth. Needless to say, only the male piglets underwent this surgery. Just as in the clipping of a young pig's teeth, the person holding the little piggy was very likely to get wet from squirts of urine, especially when Connie Ryan's sharp pen knife made an incision. After surgery each piglet was marked with shoe polish. The females were also marked with the shoe polish. Lamp oil was poured on the wound. This was done to prevent festering. I have no idea why lamp oil was used instead of some other medication. After the surgery for this litter was completed, my father usually said to Connie, "The Lord spare you your health, Connie." He replied, "And you, too, Johnny." Connie then washed his hands and lit his pipe and told a story about some unusual castration he performed in the past. As usual, he was then invited into the kitchen for a few bottles of beer and we heard more castration stories from the past.

24

KILLING PIGS

We killed our own pigs for meat. The typical farmer's dinner menu each day consisted of boiled potatoes called "spuds," boiled bacon called "mate" or "hairy bacon," and boiled cabbage. The bacon and cabbage were boiled together in the same pot and this gave a lovely flavor to the cabbage. The only day we did not have meat was Friday because of a Church Law, which required abstinence from meat on that day. On Fridays, we had fish, usually herring. I hated herring because of the bones. The bacon had a lot of fat, which I did not like. I took care of that by cautiously putting the fat into my pocket or giving it to the cat under the table. Whatever the cat did not get was later given to the dog.

Depending on the number of people in a household, a few young pigs were set aside for killing in the cold winter months. My father selected two young pigs each year. They were placed in a separate house and well fed. When the time came for killing the pigs, a day was arranged with Connie Ryan and a few neighbors who helped. When the pig was brought to the table for execution, the squealing was deafening. The pig must have known that things were not looking good! I recall one occasion when things did not go as planned and the pig got away! He was captured after a lot of effort and plenty of vulgar language. I found this very amusing watching the terrified pig trying to escape his captors. I was reminded that it was not funny.

After the pig was killed, Connie Ryan usually had a story to tell about a pig killing in the past. The pig was cleaned by pouring hot water on his body, which was shaved with sharp knives. I clearly remember the distinct odor during this procedure. When the pig was cleaned, he was placed on a ladder with his back legs tied to the top of the ladder, which was placed upright against a wall with the pig suspended from it. The pig's belly was slit open and the entrails were removed, falling into a large wicker potato basket. Then they were placed on the table to salvage what could be used for other purposes. The intestines were washed by turning them inside out for making sausages. They were turned inside out by taking one end of the intestine and folding it over and by gradually pouring water into the fold. The weight of the water caused the entire intestine to be completely turned inside out. This procedure was repeated several times until the intestine was satisfactorily cleaned. The liver, heart, and kidneys were also salvaged. But salvaging the bladder was what we as children were most interested in. The bladder was cleaned, and a straw was inserted into it to inflate it by blowing air into it. It made a nice football until it landed on thorns or got eaten by the dogs. Portions of meat from inside the pig were removed and shared with the neighbors. These neighbors in turn shared their meat with each other when they killed their pigs. The suspended pigs were securely locked in a house so that the dogs could not get to them. Before locking the door, a potato was placed in the pig's mouth to allow any remaining blood to drain out during the night.

The pig was left suspended from the ladder until the next day when it was cut into sections. After each section of meat was trimmed, it was pickled with "Salt Peter" and placed on wooden slats for another day. Next day, the sections of meat were placed in a sealed barrel, which was called a "stan" where they remained for a few weeks to soak in the pickled salt. When the sections of meat were ready to be removed from the sealed barrel, they were hung on the wall over the kitchen fire-place. They were also hung from rafters. Some sections were hung in the chimney to be smoked. Wherever the sections were hung, they remained there well preserved until they were needed for eating. When the sections were taken down for eating, they were as hard as rocks and well preserved. It is now illegal in Ireland to kill pigs in this manner. It was very cruel. They are now slaughtered at meat processing facilities.

25
_____

PADDY BOURKE'S BOAR

THE MALE PIG WHO FATHERED MANY OF THE PIGS ON OUR farm, was a boar owned by Paddy Bourke of Greenfields. His home was about three miles from my home. When a sow came in heat, we referred to it as if the sow is "piggin." Whenever we had a sow piggin, my father usually had me walk her on the three-mile journey to Paddy Bourke's boar. It was easier on the sow if she was taken in a wagon. But back then we walked everywhere, and animals did the same. The only animals that got a ride in a wagon were calves and little pigs when they were taken to the market.

The three-mile walk with a sow in heat to Paddy Bourke's boar was a slow walk, which had a few challenges. All usually went well for about a mile and a half until we crossed a bridge over a river. Just past the bridge was a steep hill. At the bottom of the hill there was a mud hole on the side of the road, which was filled with water from a little stream flowing down from the top of the hill. As soon as the sow reached this mud hole, she was tired and frothing from her mouth. She went into the mud hole and rolled around in it and got covered all over with mud and slurry. She had no intention of getting out. This caused a major delay in getting to Paddy Bourke's, which became a source of stress for me because my father had set a time limit for my return home with the sow. He had other farm tasks waiting for me and being gone too long walking the sow to and from the boar, which was a return journey of six miles, could not be used as an excuse for avoiding other assigned tasks. Imagine the stress and anxiety when walking more than one sow at the same time to Paddy Bourke's boar!

After getting the sow out of the mud hole, we walked very slowly up the steep hill. At the top of the hill, there was a four way cross roads. The challenge then was to get the sow to go straight ahead instead of turning to the left or to the right. But the sow always took one of the wrong roads, and instead of walking slowly as she had been doing, she galloped. Her recent bath in the mud hole may have given her energy! When I finally got her turned around and back to the cross roads, then off she goes on the other wrong road. It was a challenge to eventually get her on the correct road. By the time we reached Paddy Bourke's, the sow was tired and ready for another mud bath. As her luck would have it, there was always plenty of mud and slurry in Paddy Bourke's pig yard as a result of all the sows that came to mate with his very busy boar. The sow took advantage of this. Paddy Bourke came out from his house smoking his pipe saying, "I see you have another sow piggin, God bless her. Let me bring out the boar. I know he will be glad to see her." As soon as the boar saw the sow, he got all excited. But the sow usually ignored him, and so the boar got into the slurry along with her. Eventually the sow and the boar emerged from the slurry and the mating began. Paddy Bourke remarked that each time the boar blinked his eyes another young piglet was conceived.

After the sow and boar had finished mating, I set off with the sow for the three mile walk back home. As predicted, as soon as we reached the four crossroads, the sow took every wrong road and when I got her on the correct road and arrived at the mud hole, at the bottom of the hill she went in for another dip and roll. After getting her out of the mud hole, we were on our way and the sow's walk got slower. Because we had a large number of sows, I did not understand why my father did not have his own boar. It was probably less expensive to pay Paddy Bourke for the service, than to feed and maintain a boar. On arrival at home, my father was sure to ask what delayed me. On seeing the condition of the sow from rolling in the slurry and in the mud hole, I was reprimanded for allowing the sow to get into such a dirty condition. As the sow was ushered into the piggery for feeding and getting some rest, my father said, "God bless her. I hope she will have a big litter of bonhams." Then he assigned me another task.

26

THE NAIL BEHIND THE DOOR

THERE WAS A WOMAN IN MY LOCALITY WHO HAD ONE COW. She had more trouble taking care of this one cow than a farmer with a very large herd. Whenever the cow came into heat, she was serviced by a neighbor's bull. Artificial insemination of cattle was new at this time. A suggestion was made to her to have the cow artificially inseminated. She did not understand what was meant by this. It was explained to her that semen was collected from bulls on a farm at Mitchelstown Creamery, and the cows were inseminated by a man. The woman was absolutely horrified by this and wondered how this could be. Locally, this was referred to as having cows inseminated by *The Mitchelstown Bull*. The man who did the artificial insemination was referred to as *The Bull Man*. The next time the woman's cow came into heat, she decided to have her serviced by the Mitchelstown Bull. To do this, she had make a request at the local creamery. She was instructed to keep the cow in a shed and have a basin of water, a bar of soap, and a towel ready for the Bull Man who would arrive later in the day. After making her request at the creamery, she went home on her bicycle. She got everything ready for the Bull Man. She was absolutely bewildered as to how a man could inseminate a cow. This was unnatural and disgusting. She wondered what the world was coming to! But she felt she had to go along with this modern way of inseminating cows.

When the Bull Man arrived, the woman took him to the cow shed. She showed him the cow, the basin of water, the bar of soap, and the towel. Thinking to herself that the Bull Man would have to undress himself to inseminate the cow, she was not going to stay and watch. As she was leaving she told the Bull Man that here was a nail behind the door where he could hang his pants and clothes!

27
—————

HOPING THE TRAIN WILL BE LATE

DURING THE SUMMER OF 1958, A SMALL FAMILY-OWNED
carnival came to the yard of the partially demolished old school.
They stayed for three days. One of the attractions was a black
and white movie film, which was shown each night in a small
tent. The title of the film was *The Lilly of Killarney*. There was a
scene in the film where the Lilly of Killarney was undressing by
a lake before taking a swim. Just as she was about to remove a
piece of clothing, which would reveal too much, she became
hidden by a passing train. After the train had passed, the Lilly
of Killarney was swimming in the lake. At this time in rural
Ireland, some people had never been to a cinema to see a movie
film. One such man went to see this film every night for the
three nights. When asked why he was doing this, he replied
that he was hoping the train would be late this time!

28

THE CARNIVAL GIRL

DURING THE TIME WHEN THE FAMILY CARNIVAL WAS performing on the grounds of the old school, I became friendly with one of their daughters. Her name was Katie. We were both sixteen years of age at this time. My father had purchased the old school for the stones. One of my tasks was to haul away the stones on a horse and cart. Having set my eyes on Katie, I was glad to make several daily trips to the schoolyard to collect a load of stones. While loading the stones on to the cart, I had plenty of opportunity to chat with Katie. I also got friendly with her mother, and so each evening prior to the showing of the film, I was invited to help with checking the entrance tickets to the tent. When the film started and the lights were turned off, I was glad to have Katie sitting next to me!

After three days the carnival moved on to the village of Bansha, which is about twelve miles away. I was very heart broken. There was only one cure and that was to follow the carnival, so I got on my bicycle and cycled the twelve miles to Bansha. I did not tell anyone I was leaving. I arrived in time for the showing of the film. The family was surprised to see me. They asked if my family knew where I had was. I lied and said they did. So Katie's parents were not aware that they were hiding a young boy, who was missing from his home. I don't think that they suspected that I was actually chasing their daughter. Later that night when I was cycling home, I got a puncture about a mile away from the carnival. I did not want to walk the remaining eleven miles home. Neither did I want to return to the carnival family because then they would suspect that I lied about my family knowing I was at the carnival. So I spent the night in a hay barn.

Next morning when the farmer was bringing in his cows for milking, I approached him and told him about my bicycle puncture and how I spent the night in his hay barn. He felt sorry for me and took me into his house and had his wife make me a hearty breakfast and assured me that he would repair the puncture for me after he had milked his cows and delivered the milk to the creamery. By the time the puncture was repaired, it was almost midday. There was no point in going home then because I wanted to be back with my girl again that evening. When I returned to the carnival, Katie's mother quizzed me about my family allowing me to cycle to Bansha and cycle home again so late in the dark of night. Again, I lied! After the showing of the film that night, I was afraid to go home because by then I was missing for two full days. So I spent another night in the same hay barn. Next morning, I sneaked away because I did not want the farmer to see me. This would make him very suspicious. Because I was hungry and now afraid to go home, I went back to the carnival family and admitted that I had left home without telling anyone where I was. Katie's mother told me that I must go home, and they would take me after they gave me breakfast. I managed to whisper to Katie that I would be back again. Katie's father put me and my bicycle into a multi-colored van, which had carnival drawings on it, and took me home. I was glad that he brought Katie along with us.

When we arrived home my mother was very happy to see me, but my father wanted to give me a spanking. My mother stopped him by telling him to be glad that I came home safe. Katie's father also helped the situation by telling my father and mother what a good boy I was for helping his family with the seating of people for the showing of the film. Katie's father shook my hand and patted me on the head and told me to be a good boy. I was heartbroken as I watched them drive away. That was the end of my short romance with the carnival girl. My father locked my bicycle in a shed and commanded that I never leave home without his permission. That was the last time that I saw Katie. I wonder what became of her!

29

THE POSTMAN

THE POSTMAN WE HAD WHEN I WAS A CHILD RETIRED WHEN I was about seven years old. He was replaced by another post-man, who was still delivering mail to our house when I left for America some eighteen years later. He made his daily rounds delivering the mail on a bicycle. His rural route covered several miles. One of his stops was to collect letters deposited in a letterbox located in the stone wall of the old school yard. Each day the schoolchildren filled the letterbox with pebbles and waited at the wall to watch the postman get upset. When he opened the letterbox, all the pebbles fell out. When delivering an airmail letter from America, he let everyone know about it and the possibility that the envelope might contain dollars.

During the week leading up to Christmas and after Christ-mas, he usually arrived late in the evening. This was because he was offered a bottle of Guinness in every house along the way. By the time he reached our home he was not in any pain.

The day after Christmas in Ireland is known as *The Wren Day*. It is pronounced as *The "Wran" Day*. On this day, young people and some not so young, go from house to house dressed in tattered clothes turned inside out and painted faces with a dead wren or an imitation wren tied on a holly bush decorated with colored ribbons. At each house they sang or recite The Wran Song.

The wran, the wran, the king of all birds
On St. Stephen's Day was caught in the furze.
Up with the kettle and down with the pan.
Give us a penny to bury the wran.

They also sing other songs and played music. In return they are given some money. On this day, our postman, along with his wife and six children, went from house to house. They carried a decorated holly bush and an imitation wren. They had two bicycles. The postman had four children on his bicycle. One was seated on the handlebar. Another was on the crossbar. Two were seated on the rear carrier. The second child on the carrier was sitting on the handles of a hedge clippers, which had the blade inserted into the carrier. His wife had two children on her bike. On arrival at a house, the postman sang a song called, "The Jackass in the Bog," which had several verses. After the postman finished singing his song, he got a little cash and a bottle of Guinness. As the day went on and several bottles of Guinness were consumed at other houses, the number of verses in "The Jackass in the Bog" song increased!

Sometimes the postman strolled around cemeteries reading headstones. One day he was reading headstones in Solohead cemetery. The ground level of this cemetery is much higher than the road. A new grave was just opened. The gravedigger was sitting and resting against the back of the headstone of the newly opened grave. When he heard the sound of someone approaching from the other side of the headstone, he stood up and startled the postman who took off running and leaping over the wall and down on to the road below.

The local Parish Priest told me that one day when the postman was delivering mail to the priest's house, the Angelus Bell in the church was ringing. The postman was cycling his bicycle along the avenue. He was reciting the Angelus prayer. At the words, "the Word was made flesh" where it is the custom to genuflect, the postman got down from his bicycle, genuflected, and got back on his bicycle and continued on.

30
___

THE GOAT IN THE CINEMA

OCCASIONALLY, WHEN I HAD THE PRICE OF ADMITTANCE TO the cinema to see a film, and that was very seldom, I cycled the six miles to Tipperary town and joined my friends from the Christian Brothers School. One evening we came upon a goat grazing on the roadside. We kidnapped the goat and smuggled him in to the cinema under a large overcoat. Shortly after the lights were turned off and the film started, we let the goat loose out in the aisle. The goat got confused and excited and ran up and down the aisle and eventually ran on to the stage where it was clearly visible in the light coming from the projection room. People were screaming. This frightened the goat and made him more excited. Meanwhile, he was having bowel movements! The goat ran over and back across the stage a few times. Then the lights came on and the goat ran down the aisle and out the door and was never seen again. The cinema owner conducted an investigation to find out who was responsible for bringing the goat to the cinema. A few people sitting near us pointed to us as being the culprits. We were ordered to leave the cinema and banned from returning for six months.

31

MY FATHER AND THE POLICEMAN

WHENEVER MY FATHER WAS DRIVING, HE ALWAYS BECAME flustered and agitated at the sight of a policeman directing traffic. Shortly after learning to drive, on one particular Sunday morning after Mass in Tipperary Town, as he was driving down St. Michael Street toward the Main Street, he saw a policeman at the intersection of the two streets directing traffic. Because it was after Mass, the traffic on St. Michael's Street was very heavy and because there was a big hurling game in Limerick City, the traffic on the Main Street going in the direction of Limerick was also very heavy. Cautiously approaching the Main Street, and being nervous at the sight of the policemen, he put his hand out the window to signal a right-hand turn. In those days, cars did not have flashing indicator lights. Instead they had a small signal arm, which when activated popped out from the side of the car. The signal arm in the van was not working so this alone could be grounds for the policeman to issue a citation. As my father approached the intersection with his hand sticking out the window to indicate a right-hand turn, the policeman held up his hand and signaled my father to stop and wait. After a few minutes when the policeman gave the signal to proceed on into the Main Street and take a right-hand turn, my father let out the clutch too fast, which caused the van to stall. Because he was already flustered at the sight of the policeman and being a new driver, he was not yet able to restart the van without going through the long process of putting the van into neutral and putting on the handbrake. He became very excited and was fumbling with the ignition key and the starter. After he got the engine going, he again let out the clutch too fast and stalled the van a second time. The policemen got annoyed and shouted at my father to stop holding up traffic and to move on and get out of the way. My father had a hot temper and had absolutely no patience. He became so agitated with the policeman he put his head out the driver side window and shouted, "Who the ****** hell do you think you are, telling me what to do, and I was up all the ****** morning milking cows before I went to Mass while you were in your ***** bed!" He eventually got the van moving and joined the long procession of cars along the Main Street while telling us in very profane language what he thought of that policeman directing traffic without having to get out of bed in the morning and milk cows. He was lucky that the policeman did not issue a ticket to him for abusive language and perhaps a second ticket for not having a working signal indicator.

32

THE CREAMERY

CLONBRICK CREAMERY WAS A PLACE OF GREAT ACTIVITY.
Several farmers converged there every morning to deliver their
milk mostly with horses and carts, a few tractors, and a few
vans. Homes did not have television or telephones. The
creamery was where all the news was found. It was also a place
for mischief and pulling tricks on some innocent souls. My
father employed some young men to work on the farm. He was
very particular about taking care of his horses. He also had a
donkey for use by the young workers. Before he considered a
person qualified to take a horse and cart to the creamery, he had
to prove that he could manage a donkey. One of the farm
workers had great trouble at managing the donkey going to the
creamery. It was not that he was not able to manage the donkey,
but the mischief-makers at the creamery tormented him and
the donkey. They made fun of him over not being qualified to
take a horse and cart to the creamery. About the time when this
young man was almost ready to take a horse to the creamery,
the mischief-makers played a trick on him, which disqualified

him. One morning after he had emptied the milk at the creamery, he made the mistake of leaving the donkey unattended for a short time. But it was long enough to give the mischief-makers the opportunity to take the donkey out from under the cart. They put the shafts of the cart through an iron gate and reversed the donkey back between the shafts of the cart on the other side of the gate. When the young farm worker returned, he could not figure out how the donkey was tackled to the cart with the gate between them. When my father heard about this, the misfortunate young man was told that he would never be allowed to take a horse to the creamery.

33
_____

RYAN PHIL'S DONKEY

THERE WERE MANY DONKEYS GOING TO CLONBRICK creamery, but none of them were as smart as Ryan Phil's Donkey. The little donkey's name was Neddy, and what a donkey he was! The Ryan family lived about a mile and a half from the creamery. Their house was located some distance in from the road in a lane. The father of the family was Johnny, and he worked in England. His wife Katie and their children looked after the farm. Their neighbor was Pakie O'Neill, known as Rafferty O'Neill. He worked at the creamery. Each morning after Katie Ryan and her family had milked their cows, they sent Neddy the Donkey off to the creamery on his own pulling a cart loaded with churns of milk. The Creamery Book for recording the amount of milk supplied to the creamery was placed under the handle of a lid of one of the milk churns. When the donkey passed the school, we, as children, said loudly, "There goes Phil's Ass." Our teacher, Mrs. Pidge O'Donovan, ordered us to be quiet.

When the donkey arrived at the creamery, he was met by

Rafferty O'Neill, who guided him to the platform to have the milk emptied into the large milk vats and the amount of gallons recorded in the little creamery book, which was kept under the handle of the lid in one of the churns. Then he brought the donkey to the other end of the creamery and filled up the churns with skim milk. When everything was ready, Rafferty O'Neill gave the little donkey a slap on his backside and sent him on his way home again. When the donkey passed the school on his way home, the children again loudly said, "There goes Phil's Ass again." This little donkey spent many years going to the creamery and coming from the creamery on his own. He always stayed on his correct side of the road and always knew when to turn into the laneway leading to his home.

On one occasion, the little donkey was pulling the cart along the road as usual, without anyone in charge of him. A local policeman on his bicycle came upon him. The policeman knew who owned the donkey. So he issued a summons to Katie Ryan, charging her with violating the law by having donkey pulling a loaded cart on a public road with no person in charge. When Katie Ryan appeared in court, the judge asked the policeman if the donkey was on his correct side of the road. The policeman replied that the donkey was on the correct side of the road. The judge said, "This little donkey clearly knows the rules of the road, and I can't say that for some human beings. This case is dismissed!" The local weekly newspaper, The Nationalist, carried this story the following week commending Neddy the Donkey for his knowledge of the rules of the road.

34

WHERE IS THE TOILET?

IN THE EARLY 1960S, WE DID NOT HAVE RUNNING WATER IN our house. This meant we did not have a toilet in the house. My brother, P.J., was working in London. His supervisor, who was a West Indian, took a holiday in Ireland and made an unexpected visit to my home. My mother, who was all alone in the house at the time, heard a knock on the door and went to answer it. When she opened the door and saw the West Indian standing there, she got a terrible fright. This was the first time in her life that she had met a person with dark skin. The visitor introduced himself as being from London, and that he was my brother P.J.'s supervisor. When my mother regained her composure, she nervously invited this strange looking man to come in. Upon entering the kitchen, the very first words out of his mouth were, "Where is the toilet?" My mother got all flustered and took him to her bedroom. With a trembling hand, she pulled out the chamber pot from under the bed and handed it to the West Indian and left the room while the unusual visitor relieved himself.

Later that day when my father came home my mother asked him to sit down to hear what she had to tell him. She told him about the very strange looking man with very dark skin and white teeth and white eyes, who introduced himself as being P.J.'s supervisor, and how she invited him in. Then she went on to tell him about the West Indian asking for the toilet. On hearing this, my father took off his hat and in a loud voice exclaimed, "Wasn't it far he brought his pee with him? Why didn't he make it before he left London?"

35

THE MONK'S SHOP

PADDY MYRICK WAS KNOWN LOCALLY AS "THE MONK." HE dressed in black clothes and wore a black hat. His mode of transport was a pony and cart. He was seated facing forward on a plank secured to the two wooden wheel guards of the cart, which were called "cripples." He had a little shop situated between the old school and the bridge over the river in Ayle. Being so close to the river, the floor in his little house was sometimes under water. It was a very small shop, which had a very short counter at the end of the kitchen. The house had very small windows and so it was dimly lit even in daylight. The only items he sold were lamp oil, bread, tea and sugar, and an assortment of candy or sweets such. The assortment of sweets consisted of: Peggy's Legs, Gob Stoppers, Bull's Eyes, Penny Bars, and Black Jack Licorice known as "Cat's Cuckeys." During lunchtime at school, whenever we had a penny or two, which was very seldom, we went to The Monk's Shop. Because the house was very dimly lit and the Monk had bad eyesight, when we had no money, we tried to trick him by giving him a little holy medal. Whenever the Monk realized it was a medal, he shouted and ordered the cheater out of the shop with a warning not to return again. The assortment of candy was on display in jars on the counter top and on the ledge of the very small window. The Monk's cat was usually stretched out sleeping on top of the candy. This did not bother us. We were delighted to get the sweets, and we did not mind removing the cat's hair.

When the Monk's cat was not sitting on the sweets in the window, he was sleeping by the fireside in the Monk's shop. The Monk was very proud of the fact that he had trained the cat to obey certain commands. One command the Monk gave to the cat was. "Cat, cat, lay down and show me your cuckey." The cat rolled over on his back and spread his back legs and showed off his equipment! The Monk took great delight in this demonstration!

The Monk was found dead one afternoon in the field behind his house with a bundle of firewood and a billhook next to him. When we arrived at school next morning, we cried when we got the news of the Monk's death. There was a procession of children lined up to enter the house and pay our respects. Each child cried as he or she stood by the Monk's corpse, which was laid out in a bed located in an alcove in the wall of a very small bedroom. All day long in school children were sobbing and crying because The Monk was dead. Our teacher, Mrs. Pidge O'Donovan, had us pray for the happy repose of The Monk's soul. She then very sternly told us that if we had ever tried to deceive The Monk by giving him a medal for sweets instead of money that we had to tell it to the priest in confession.

36

ELECTION DAY

On Election Day, my father drove elderly voters to the polling station at Ayle School. He made sure that everyone knew that he was a staunch Fine Gael supporter. So only those who promised to vote for Fine Gael candidates, were entitled to be taken by him to the polling station. Of course, everyone promised, but he suspected that many of them would promise anything in order to get a ride! On Election Day, before taking voters to the polling station, he had to take milk to Clonbrick Creamery in his van. He had Fine Gael posters all over the outside of the van. Rafferty O'Neill, who worked at the creamery, was a staunch Fianna áil supporter and was always up to mischief. One particular Election Day, and unknown to my father, Rafferty O'Neill placed Fianna Fáil posters on the passenger side of the van. After my father had finished his creamery business, he spent several hours driving people to the polling station with Fine Gael posters on the driver's side of the van and Fianna Fáil posters on the other side. Eventually a Fianna Fáil supporter, who was greatly amused by this, brought it to my father's attention. With great glee, he asked my father which party he supported. My father, knowing that everyone knew which party he supported, took great offence at being asked such a ridiculous question and reprimanded this person for this. The Fianna Fáil supporter then took great pleasure in pointing out to my father the Fianna Fail posters on the side of the van. My father could not believe what he saw and became very agitated and immediately suspected that Rafferty O'Neill was the culprit.

37

THE FORGE

Tom Browne had a forge at the Cross of Moanrue. His brother Richard also worked there. The forge was not only a place where horses were shoed and iron bands were made for timber wheels and farm machinery repaired, but it was also a great meeting place to get all the news of the day. Wet days were always very busy days at the forge because farm work stopped when it was raining. I can recall the sound of the hammer striking the hot iron on the anvil as Tom Browne shaped the horseshoes. The glowing fire was fanned by a large bellows, which was operated by pulling a swing stick. As Tom Browne pulled on the bellows with one hand, his other hand was turning the iron in the fire. The floor of the forge had large wooden planks, which were worn thin by the hoofs of many horses down through the years.

38
___

THE PUCK GOAT

A LOCAL FAMILY HAD A MALE GOAT, WHICH WAS USED AS A stud. They had a hand-painted sign, which advertised the availability of the goat for service. The sign read as follows:

UZ HAS A PUCK
UZ CHARGE A SHILLIN
FOR A RUT
IF RUT NOT WORK
UZ CHARGE NOTTEN
FOR NUDDER RUT

39

THE MAN IN THE BOX

THERE WAS A MAN, WHO TRAVELLED THE LOCAL RURAL ROADS in a box with three wheels in the late 1940s, when there was hardly any motor traffic. I never knew his name. He was known to me as The Man in the Box. He served in the British Army during The Second World War and lost both of his legs. I have no idea how he managed to get in or out of the box or how he managed when nature called! He sat upright in the box and wore a hat. He propelled his box along the road with a stick in each hand, which was in the shape of a gavel or a small mallet. He used to stop at the gate to our farmhouse and talk with my grandmother. He had a pack of cigarettes under an oil sheet cloth, which covered whatever was left of his legs. As soon as he stopped to talk with my grandmother, he pulled out his pack of cigarettes and lit up. As soon as he finished his smoke, he pushed off going wherever he was going. To turn his box to the left or right he leaned back and raised up the single wheel in front and guided the box in the direction he wished to go.

One night he was having a drink in a local pub. He was at

ground level sitting in his box. Some locals were making fun of him. The Man in the Box was not amused. He motioned to one of the men to stoop down, indicating that he wanted to whisper something to him. When the man bent down, the Man in the Box grabbed him by the neck and wrestled him to the ground while maintaining a chokehold. The Man in the Box had developed very strong wrists from pushing his little box cart along the road using the gavel or small mallet shaped sticks. When the onlookers in the pub saw the strength of the Man in the Box, and how he wrestled an agile man to the floor, nobody ever again made fun of him.

40

BOLD BOYS

THERE WAS AN ELDERLY MAN IN THE LOCALITY, WHO LIVED
alone. He lived in a thatched cottage, which was very small. He
had a thick white moustache. Because he smoked a pipe, his
moustache had streaks of brown and yellow. He kept a few
geese in a small plot behind his cottage. He also kept a donkey
and a cart. The cart had wooden wheels. Each day he walked
though fields collecting firewood, which he brought home, tied
up in a bundle on his back. Whenever he was absent from his
house, he never locked his door. This offered an opportunity for
some mischief.

On one occasion while he was out collecting firewood, we
caught a few of the geese and brought them into the house.
Then we went hiding in the bushes, anxiously awaiting the reaction of the elderly man when he returned. In the meantime, the
geese got up on the kitchen table to feast on whatever they
could eat. They also left their droppings all over the house.
When the old man returned, he went into a rage. He was
cursing and swearing and saying what he would do with the

little brats who did this. This caused the cackling geese to get flustered and flap their wings trying to escape. Because they were so excited and frightened, they did not see the open door to get out. A few of them went toward the light, which was the kitchen window, and crashed into the glass. This caused them to deposit more droppings. They broke the window getting out. We bad boys, disappeared out of sight before the old man saw us.

On another occasion while the old man was out collecting firewood, we removed the timber wheels from the cart. Then we turned the cart on its side and maneuvered it into the house. We put the wheels back under it and brought in the donkey and tackled him and hooked him up to the cart. We tied him to one of the legs of the kitchen table. Then we waited in hiding for the return of the old man. When he returned, he got a terrible fright when he saw the donkey and cart and the donkey tied to a leg of the kitchen table. He got so angry that we got frightened and left the scene while it was safe. Word of this mischief spread all around the locality. Some people were amused by it. But most people were angry that a bunch of brats did this to an old man. They were determined to catch the culprits. From then on, we did not get into any more mischief like this.

41

FLEA POWDER IN BED

IT WAS A PRACTICE IN THE FARMING COMMUNITY TO HAVE the children spend several days with cousins to help with the farm work. Households rotated having each other's children spend a few days at a time. On one of these exchanges, we were staying with the O'Malley family of Towerhill, Cappamore. John O'Malley was a first cousin of my father. He and his wife, Kathleen, lived in a lovely single-story thatched house. John O'Malley and his wife slept in a room on the ground floor directly off the kitchen. We slept in an attic room overhead, which had a very small window at the gable end. Out in the pig house we spotted a tin of D.D.T. This was a powder, which was used to shake on pigs to kill fleas and ticks.

When we got an opportunity, we emptied the entire tin of the flea powder between the bed sheets of the bed of John and Kathleen O'Malley. We went up to bed that night very apprehensive about the consequences of this prank. But like other pranks, we figured it was going to be fun when John and Kathleen O'Malley got in between the saturated flea powder sheets of their bed. We left our room door open and stayed alert. John O'Malley got into his bed and inhaled the flea powder. He screamed an unmerciful roar, which gave his wife such a fright that she also screamed thinking he might have been bitten by a rat in the bed. He jumped out of the bed with his face and long-john underwear covered with flea powder. He cried out that he was going kill those little brats. When we heard him coming up the stairs, we made a dash for the very small window to escape. Wearing no clothes, we jumped about fifteen feet to the ground outside. Now that we were outside, we were afraid to come in. We spent the night sleeping in the hayshed in our bare bottoms. For the next several days we had to keep our distance from John O'Malley to avoid his wrath.

42

HENNESSEY'S WELL

WE SPENT A CONSIDERABLE AMOUNT OF TIME AT HENNESSY'S of Lisobyhane, Emly. This was the birthplace of my grandmother, Sarah Hennessy. There was an open well in the yard, which was eighty feet deep. Water was drawn from the well by means of a bucket attached to a rope, which was rolled around a roller with a handle. The bucket was battered from constant contact with the wall of the well when it was lowered or being withdrawn from the well. There were times when adults were not watching us, we took turns being lowered into the well by getting into the bucket while holding on to the rope. Our young minds did not see how dangerous this was. Eventually we were caught in the act, and the well was secured with a cover, which was locked.

43

TEARS AND DRINK

Timmy Duggan of Barnaleen was a second cousin of my father. His brother Tom, who left Ireland for Canada, returned home for a holiday sometime in the late 1950s. When the time came for his return to Canada, my father thought it would be nice if our family went to Shannon Airport to see him off. None of us had ever been to Shannon Airport or seen a plane on the ground.

When Tom Duggan and his wife had checked in, we all went to the bar for a drink. Timmy Duggan had a few drinks and was getting very sentimental over the departure of his brother Tom. When it was time to board, there were hand-shakes and hugs and tears and a promise to return again.

It was a nighttime flight, and the airport at that time was very small. There was an observation balcony on the roof from which one could see the passengers boarding the plane. We all went up to the observation deck and watched Tom Duggan and his wife walk toward the plane. When Tom Duggan got to the top of the stairwell, he turned around and waved back to us.

Timmy Duggan shouted some profanities lamenting Tom's departure and started crying. Then my father started to cry, and everyone was crying.

The plane was an Air Canada with four propeller engines. Each engine started up, and the plane eventually moved away. After it took off, Timmy Duggan and all of us headed to the bar. After several drinks and much crying over the possibility that Tom Duggan would never again return, it was time to go home. Timmy Duggan and my father were very drunk. Timmy Duggan never drove a car, but he had Mick O'Dwyer, known as Mick the Bun, as his driver. My father was too drunk to drive, and I was only about sixteen years of age, so he said I had to drive home. I had never before driven on the road. I did not have a driving license. At that time, most of the police got around on bicycles, and there were very few patrol cars. So the odds of being stopped by the police, was not a concern. We all got home safely.

44

THE FAMILY ROSARY

When I left Ireland for America in 1967, The Rosary was recited every night in most homes, especially in rural Ireland. In my home, it was recited either after supper or after the nine o'clock news on the radio. We did not have television at that time. We sat around the open fire. When it was time to recite The Rosary, we got down on our knees with our elbows on the chair and our backs to the fire. My father usually led The Rosary. He designated who would lead each decade. It was always good to get one of the early decades because one might have dozed off by the time a later decade was recited.

My father began with the Apostles Creed followed by The Lord's Prayer, three Hail Mary's, and the Glory Be to The Father. Each family member then took their turn at leading the particular assigned decade. Sometimes, when it was someone's turn to lead a decade, that person may have dozed off. My father would then shout, "Whose turn is it? Wake up." At other times, the person leading the decade might come up short on the ten Hail Mary's. My father would say, "Keep going." If the person leading the decade exceeded the ten Hail Mary's, my father would say, "Stop, stop." There were often times when something silly happened during The Rosary, and one could get a fit of giggling which could not be controlled. This annoyed my father. By then, there was no sense of prayerfulness, but the intentions were good!

Following the five decades of The Rosary came the recitation of the Hail Holy Queen, followed by the Litany of the Blessed Virgin Mary. Then came what was known as "The Trimmings." This was a long list of Hail Mary's for various intentions. Typical were individual Hail Mary's for the happy repose of departed souls; many of them dead for several years. This list got longer and longer each year. One Hail Mary for all the departed souls was not enough. Each one got a separate Hail Mary. Following the prayers for departed souls came a separate Hail Mary for a long list of intentions. Typical were good weather, a cow expected to have a calf that night, or a good price for the pigs at the market next day. The list went on and on. When my sister Nuala was a child, she requested a Hail Mary for Santa Claus! The trimmings were exhausting!

If a neighbor happened to drop in while The Rosary was being recited, he or she got down on his or her knees and joined in. By the time The Rosary and the trimmings ended, there was always one or two persons sound asleep with elbows and face resting on the chair. Then it was time to make tea before going to bed.

45
___

THE EASTER DUTY

PRIOR TO THE SECOND VATICAN COUNCIL OF 1962 TO 1965, reception of Holy Communion was less frequent than it is today. The Church had to impose a law, which made it mandatory to receive at least once a year during the Easter Season. This became known as The Easter Duty. Two of the reasons for the infrequent reception were not feeling worthy and long fasting hours prior to reception.

Up until the time I began my studies for the priesthood, my father received Communion only once a year during the Easter Season. Once I began study for the priesthood, he went twice a year. He considered that as the father of a future priest, he should do this! People felt they were not worthy to receive. For example, on the one Sunday in the year when my father went to Holy Communion, he did not go the following day if that day was a Holy Day of obligation. He felt that he was unable to keep himself "right" for two successive days. There were also the fasting regulations. One had to fast from midnight of the night before reception. For my father, this was very stressful.

He had to rise in the morning around five o'clock to milk cows. Then deliver milk to the creamery. Mass was at eleven o'clock. By the time, he arrived home it was around one o'clock in the afternoon. By then, he was starving with hunger and had a split-ting headache. As well as all that, he had to struggle all morning to refrain from using profane language when cows did not coop-erate. If he had an outburst, he did not consider himself "right" to receive and had to start all over again on another Sunday.

There was also the added requirement of having to go to confession prior to the reception of Holy Communion. This was a major undertaking. He would ask my mother to check the entry in the previous year's calendar to see what date he went to confession. The problem was that calendar was already discarded so he had no idea when it was. After going to confes-sion, the entire household entered a period of silence so as not to upset "Daddy, who would be receiving in the morning." When it came time for milking cows the morning of reception of Communion, my father stayed in the house until all the cows were in place. This helped him to refrain from profane words when the cows did not behave.

Following the Second Vatican Council, the fasting laws were changed to just one hour before Communion, and the Church placed more emphasis on how much God loves us instead of constantly dwelling on the aspect of being unworthy. With this change, my father was able to receive Holy Communion more frequently. He went twice a year! Before he died in 1981, he received Holy Communion once every month.

46

A BLIND DOG NAMED CUSH

MY PATERNAL GREAT-GRANDMOTHER WAS MARGARET Deegan. Her brother, Tom Deegan, and his wife, Nora Godfrey, had a blind dog named Cush. The dog never left the farmyard. One Saturday, Tom Deegan was returning home from Tipperary town on his horse and cart. When crossing a bridge over a stream about a mile from his home, the blind dog Cush jumped up on the cart and then vanished.

When Tom Deegan got home, he asked his wife if Cush had been out. She replied that the dog was sleeping in front of the fireplace all day. He told his wife about Cush jumping up on the cart at the bridge and suddenly vanishing. She assured him that the dog never left the house all day.

The following Saturday, when Tom Deegan was on his way home again from Tipperary town on his horse and cart, he died suddenly crossing the bridge at the exact same spot where the blind dog, Cush, jumped up on the cart the previous Saturday. The blind dog, Cush, lived on for a few more years and continued sleeping by the fireside.

47

FAMILY EVICTION

ON MAY 10, 1889, WHEN MY GREAT GRANDFATHER WAS A tenant farmer, he was evicted by the landlord for failure to pay his rent for the land. When an eviction took place, the landlord had the household furniture thrown out on the roadside and demolished the house. On the day that my great grandfather was evicted, his wife was sick in bed. As she lay in bed, the house was demolished around her, but her bedroom was left intact. My grandfather, who was living with my great-grandfather, was 25 years of age at that time. He was very upset over the eviction and decided to shoot the landlord. He enlisted the help of a twenty-year-old neighbor, whose father and mother were also evicted on that same day of May 10, 1889.

On the day following the eviction, they went to the house of the landlord. They could see the landlord sitting at a table. They fired shots through a window. The pellets from the gunfire greased the right side of the landlord's neck. Because of the two evictions of the previous day, he suspected who the culprits might be. The neighbor was blamed and arrested. He was tried in court. He was not convicted because there was no evidence to prove who fired the shots. My grandfather was still determined to punish the landlord. A few days after the court and the acquittal of the neighbor, he drove up the road on a horse and cart. He took with him a rifle and a supply of bullets. On reaching the gate of the avenue into the landlord's house, he stopped the horse and cart. He stood up on the cart and fired several shots into the air. Then as cool as a breeze, he turned the horse and cart around and went home. His father eventually paid the rent and regained possession of the land.

48

THE CROSSROADS

In rural areas, local people gathered at their local crossroads on Sunday afternoons and on the long daylight evenings during summer. They enjoyed being together to chat and catch up on news. Some mischief also took place, such as placing live frogs in someone's pocket as well as other pranks. A game of skittles was usually played. This consisted of drawing a circle or a diamond with a cross on the inside. It was drawn with chalk on the road surface. Five pins, which were about two inches in height, were placed upright on the circle or diamond. Four of the pins were placed on each of the four corners of the diamond. The fifth pin was placed on the center of the cross. The pins were made from cut-off sections of a handle from a shovel or pitchfork. Each of the four pins had a numerical value of one to four. The pin in the center had the numerical value of five.

Outside of the diamond or circle, was a line drawn, which was one foot away from the diamond or circle. A cut-off shovel or fork handle about a foot in length was placed on top of the

99

line. This was called a breaker. About three yards back from the breaker was a line, which indicated where the player had to stand. The player had three small logs of about a foot in length. These logs were known as blogs. The object of the game was to throw one blog at a time to knock out the five pins within the circle or diamond. The knocked pins had to be completely outside of the circle or diamond. The score was tallied on the numerical value of the pins, which were knocked outside of the circle or diamond. The challenge was that when throwing a blog, it had to hit the ground forward of the breaker. Otherwise, any pins knocked would not count. Individuals competed with each other to achieve the highest score.

Back then there was very little road traffic. Occasionally, when a car came along, it usually knocked over all the pins. This caused a lot of grief for an individual who was scoring well. He had to start all over again and maybe did not score as well as in the previous round. There was a lot of fun at those crossroad gatherings. Occasionally, at some crossroads there was music and dancing. Those happy days are long gone. There was no television and some people did not even have a radio. The crossroad was the place to go to. Sadly, there are no gatherings at the crossroads anymore.

49

JACKIE BREEN'S CAR

JACKIE BREEN WAS AN ELDERLY UNMARRIED FARMER, WHO lived alone. He was very set in his ways. His mode of transport was on a bicycle or on the back of a farm horse without a saddle. He was very good at training farm horses. This man always wore hobnail boots and walked with a long stride. He shaved his face with an open razor without the aid of a mirror, or a looking glass, as he called it. On several occasions when in his house to drive him somewhere, I saw him shave without a mirror. He did not even have a mirror in his house. When I offered to get one for him, he was adamant about not wanting such an item. He had not seen his face in a mirror since he was a child. He said that he remembered how his face looked. He had no desire to see if his face had changed down through the years since he last saw it as a child in a broken mirror his parents had. It was a study to watch him shave with an open razor without using a mirror.

Jackie Breen was a man who minded his own business and did not want anyone else to know his business. My father was probably the only person that he confided in. One night he arrived at my home and chatted away with my father about farming matters. When it came time for him to leave, he asked my father to come outside with him because he had something to tell him and did not want anyone else to know about it. We were wondering what the big secret could be. Was he getting married, and if he was, who would want to marry such a contrary old man! If he was getting married, would he let the wife have a mirror or a looking glass? What could the big secret be? My father returned after about a half hour looking very solemn. He sat there in silence looking into the fire. Eventually, he could not keep the secret to himself any longer. He told us that he had an announcement to make, and that what he was going to tell us was absolutely confidential and not a word was to be said outside of the house. We all drew close to my father for the announcement.

My father always wore a hat. The only times he removed it was when going to bed, in church, saying his prayers, eating his meals, and whenever he was making a solemn announcement. He removed his hat. Slowly and distinctly, he told us that Jackie Breen was just after buying a motorcar! We were all stunned. We could not imagine Jackie Breen, with his heavy hobnail boots, trying to drive a car. When I asked who was going to teach him how to drive, my father replied that Jackie Breen wanted him, or me, to teach him. My father insisted that he could not do it because neither one of them had enough patience with each other. By default, I was designated to be the teacher. When I asked about the make and model of the car, I was told that Jackie Breen had no idea about that. All he could tell was that it had four wheels and was black. I was also told that the car was purchased at a garage in Cahir, which was about fifteen miles away. It seems that Jackie Breen had cycled the fifteen miles each way on that day to purchase the car. He did not want to shop locally because he did not want any local person to know his business. I was also told that my father and Jackie Breen had arranged for the car to be collected the following day.

The following day, my father drove Jackie Breen and myself to collect the car. On the way to the garage, Jackie Breen was asking my father questions about driving, such as how to make the car go faster or slower. But it was like talking to a wall. Jackie had no idea or understanding of my father's explanations. On arrival at the garage, I discovered that the car was an Austin A 30. This model was commonly known as a "Baby Austin." It was a used car with the registration number of OIK 755. This was a Dublin registration. The garage owner suggested that I take the car for a test drive. Jackie Breen, my father, and the garage owner came along for the ride. Everything was going grand, and the car was lovely to drive. But about two miles out the main road going toward Clonmel, the car stalled. We had run of out petrol! There was no petrol pump between the garage and where we were. When things went wrong, my father always used the expression, "Praised be to God Almighty, what is wrong now." He repeated this several times as we sat there in the car while traffic was trying to overtake us. He gave the garage owner an earful about taking us for a drive on an empty petrol tank. There was nothing else we could do but turn the car around while dodging the traffic going both ways and push the car all the way back to the garage, which was uphill in some places. When we arrived back at the garage, the owner filled up the petrol tank at no charge as a gesture to make up for what had happened.

My father went on home, and I followed in the car with Jackie Breen as my companion. Along the way, he was asking questions about operating a car. When I informed him that he had to get a driving license, he did not understand why. We also had to get the car insured. This was all news to him. We got this done the following day. At that time in Ireland, a driving test was not required to obtain a license. A few days later, the driving lessons began. The first task was to explain to him the function of the clutch, brake, and accelerator. That was exhausting! Next came an explanation of the gears and how to find each gear including reverse. He could not understand why the gear lever had to be moved from side-to-side instead of just up or down. After some time at this session, he decided that he had enough for one day and needed to clear his head.

The real challenge started a few days later when he agreed to take another lesson. In the interest of safety, it was best to take the car out into a field. Because of his wearing big hobnailed boots, it was difficult to operate the clutch and the accelerator. When he put his foot on the accelerator, he pushed it all the way to the floor. Letting out the clutch gradually was not going to happen. Finally, after several attempts, we got moving in first gear with the accelerator all the way to the floor. He kept looking down at his feet instead of looking ahead. Suddenly we were heading straight for an electric pole, and I yelled at him to turn the steering wheel to avoid a collision. He turned the wheel so much that we did a complete horseshoe turn, which almost caused the car to overturn. We just missed hitting the electric pole by only a few feet. To regain my composure, I told him to press in on the clutch and use the brake pedal to stop. He hit the pedal so hard that we came to an abrupt stop, and the engine stalled. Jackie Breen decided there and then that he had enough of adventure for one day. I felt the same way! He insisted on leaving the car where it was there in the field. We walked away from the car, and he said he would wait until the following week for another lesson. About a week later, I gave him another lesson. This was no more successful than the lesson of the previous week. Because I could not get him to stop looking down at his feet, I took the car to another field, which did not have any poles. This time we almost ended up in a ditch! He got so disgusted at his failure to make any progress that he gave up on the idea of taking any further instructions. I pleaded with him not to give up. He agreed to try again later on. But that never happened. Whenever I asked him to take another lesson, his reply was that he would do so at another time.

He suggested that in the meantime that I should use the car and that I could drive him on some errands. All this took place during my second year in study for the priesthood. To make a long story short, I had the use of Jackie Breen's car during my Christmas and summer holidays from college for the following four years. He did not want to sell the car because he had intended to learn to drive at some time in the future. He continued to tax and insure the car and pay for any maintenance expenses. How lucky could I be! But I had one problem with using the car. I had no money for petrol. My father did not give us any cash allowance, so I was constantly broke. But I found a solution to the problem.

Whenever my father filled up his van with petrol, I waited for the opportunity to siphon a few bottles of petrol from the van and into the car. When my father was away from the house and maybe out in the fields, I had a one-pint whiskey bottle and an old tube from the milking machine.

I used to put the tube into the petrol tank of my father's van and siphon out a few whiskey bottles of petrol for the car. My father would not miss a few whiskey bottles of petrol, but I would be greatly blessed by the precious liquid. However, my father did make an observation about the fact that he was getting low mileage recently from a tank of petrol. I assured him that this was probably because he was recently trans-porting heavy sacks of potatoes up steep hills in low gear, and that this increased the consumption of petrol. But he was sharp enough to counter respond that he was transporting heavy sacks of potatoes all year round, and that it was only during my holidays that he had to fill the petrol tank more frequently! When I meet him in Heaven I must ask him if he suspected that I was stealing petrol from his van. May God forgive me!

Jackie Breen never got around to learning to drive a car. After I left for America in 1967, the car got very little use. In time, it began to rust and was eventually parked permanently in the yard at my home. Whenever I returned to Ireland for a holiday, Jackie Breen was still riding his bicycle and did so until he died. He continued to shave without a mirror or a looking glass and never saw his image since the last time he saw it as a child in his parent's broken mirror. The car is now rusted out, and I have the registration plate OIK 755, which I removed from the car.

50
THE CHICKEN IN THE EGG

FROM A VERY YOUNG AGE, MY BROTHER, OWEN ROE, FOUND various ways to be financially independent. Some of his projects were collecting beer bottles, and getting a penny for each of them at a local public house. Sometimes he took some of those bottles home with him and returned them at a later date to sell them again. Another one of his projects was removing the skin from dead cows and calves, and selling it at a tannery in Tipperary town. But his most profitable project was in the business of selling eggs.

He collected eggs by visiting local farmers and asking them if he could take a look inside their henhouses. He told them that his father was planning to expand his henhouse and needed some ideas for this. Permission was always granted to enter the henhouses and take a look around. But my brother was looking for something else in the henhouses instead of new ideas for building a henhouse!

While inside the henhouse he checked the boxes where the hens had laid their eggs. He placed a few eggs in his pockets and then moved on to another henhouse and did the same thing. My mother frequently remarked that her hens were not laying plentiful amounts of eggs. She never copped on to the fact that her son was stealing the eggs. When my brother had collected a dozen eggs, he took them to a local grocery store in the village where he sold them as fresh eggs at market price. This moneymaking project was very successful for some time.

There was an elderly man in the village that liked a fresh boiled egg with his breakfast every morning. He purchased one fresh egg each evening at the grocery store. Because my brother was the only supplier of daily fresh eggs, it was more than likely that he supplied the eggs, which the elderly man purchased. One morning, the elderly man arrived at the grocery store in a rage. He complained that after he removed the shell from the egg that morning, he was horrified to find a chicken in it!! The storeowner apologized and told the elderly man the name of the young lad who supplied the fresh eggs. The elderly man was raging and swore that he would never again purchase eggs or anything else at that store. Now the storeowner was raging because he had lost a long-time valuable customer. When my brother arrived later that day with his daily supply of eggs, the store owner in anger told him about the chicken in the elderly man's egg and ordered him to leave the village immediately and never come back to that store again. My brother's egg business collapsed all because he put his hand into the egg box of a hatching hen. Word spread that the elderly man told everyone that he would never again have a boiled egg with his breakfast. My mother's hens were laying plenty of eggs again!

51

THE TINKER'S HORSES

HORSE TRADING WAS A WAY OF LIFE AND A SOURCE OF INCOME for the tinkers in Ireland. Horse-drawn caravans travelled the roads, with several horses following on. The horses usually grazed along the side of the roads wherever the tinkers set up camp. They also availed of local farmers fields to graze their horses during the dark of night. My father got very annoyed when he found horses in one of his fields in the morning when rounding up the cows for milking. Sometimes he just put the horses out in the road. At other times, he took more drastic action. He had two favorite remedies.

One remedy was to place a boiling hot potato up under the horse's tail next to the rectum. The horse responded by squeezing his tail so tight that the potato really burned the horse's rectum. The horse then took off in a mad gallop with his tail tightly pressed between his legs. The horse did not have enough sense to lift his tail and let the potato drop. This is what we could call no horse sense!

Another remedy was to tie an empty paint can to the end of

the horse's tail. When the horse took off running, the empty paint can kept hitting his back legs, which frightened him. This made the horse gallop at great speed and kick up his back legs. In both cases, whether it was the hot boiled potato, or the empty paint can, the horse galloped at excessive speed for several miles before stopping from exhaustion. As a child, I was highly amused and entertained by all this. When word of my father's remedies for getting rid of houses grazing in his fields spread among the tinker people, they stopped grazing their horses in our fields.

52

THE TINKER'S DINNER

ONE DAY WHEN MY FATHER WAS HAVING HIS DINNER, A tinker man came to the door of our house. He wanted to see if my father was interested in buying a horse from him. On that day, my father was extremely busy with work and could use more help. He told the tinker man that he was not interested in buying a horse. He then asked the tinker man if he would help him with the work.

The tinker man, smelling the dinner cooking inside, told my father that his belly was empty, and that he was unable to help because an empty bag could not stand upright. My father then offered to share his dinner with the tinker in exchange for his help with the work. The tinker agreed and was invited in to sit at the table for dinner. He had a ferocious appetite!

When the dinner was finished, my father invited the tinker man to go with him to work as agreed before the dinner. The tinker man replied that his belly was now very full like a stuffed bag, and that a full bag could not bend, and in that condition, he was unable to work! My father was speechless at what the tinker man just said! He got very annoyed and told him never to appear again in the locality. The tinker man went his way, smiling with a full belly, and my father went back to work in disbelief that he had been fooled by the hungry tinker man.

53

THE THRESHING DAY

IN THE LOCALITY WHERE I GREW UP, MOST FARMERS GREW about an acre of oats to feed the horses. A few farmers also grew wheat and barley, which was for sale. At my home, we planted oats only. My father had his own seed sower, which was pulled by two horses. When the seeds were planted in the ground, the birds of the air tried to scratch up the grain and eat it. The way to prevent this was to place upright sticks in the ground with black sewing thread strung from them across the entire garden. The sight of a few birds dangling by their legs from a thread with their wings flapping frightened other birds away.

When the crop was ripe, it was cut by a reaper and binder. This machine tied the straw into bundles called sheaves. The sheaves were stacked and the straw was given time to dry out. Later on the sheaves were loaded on to a horse and cart and brought to the farmyard where they were stacked into larger stacks in preparation for the threshing. The large stacks were strategically placed in such a way that the threshing machine could be parked between them. When the day came for the threshing, neighboring farmers arrived to help with the work. Each of those farmers had their own day for threshing, and the same neighbors helped. It was a rotation system where several local farmers helped each other. Usually about twenty local farmers and farm helpers were on hand to help at each threshing.

Threshing day was a very busy day on the farm. The workmen had to be fed, and this was a major undertaking for the housewife. She enlisted several other local women to help with the cooking, all of which was done over an open fire before the advent of rural electrification. Additional tables were borrowed from neighboring houses. Additional silverware and dishes and mugs were also borrowed. Feeding a team of about twenty hungry men meant that a few sacks of potatoes had to be boiled. Home cured bacon had to be boiled along with plenty of cabbage. It was an enormous task for any housewife. She, in turn, helped her neighboring housewives on their threshing day. The farmer had to make sure to have plenty of drink on hand for thirsty men. From the local public house, he procured a barrel of Guinness stout and several bottles of lemonade for the children who were helping. On threshing day, children from that household were excused from attending school. Because Irish weather was unpredictable, the farmer was constantly looking at the sky hoping for a sunny day. He was anxious to have his grain threshed and safely stored away to feed his horses during the coming year.

Before the threshing began, there was plenty of other work to be done. Cows had to be milked, and the milk had to be delivered to the creamery. Calves had to be fed, as well as pigs. To add to the pressure, that might be that very morning that a pregnant sow decided to deliver her new born piglets. This was where the children who are home from school could help. When the time drew near for the threshing machine to arrive, men were arriving from different directions. Some arrived on bicycles. Others arrived walking from across the fields. A few others arrived on horse and carts. They were needed to take the sacks of grain to the barn for storage. While waiting for the threshing machine to arrive, the men gathered around and chatted and shared the latest news they got at the creamery that morning. In the midst of all this, the farmer arrived on a horse and cart with a barrel of Guinness stout. An important item to accompany the barrel of Guinness was a tap known as a "cock." This was inserted into one end of the barrel for draining the contents. When the cock was in place, the barrel was turned on its side ready for use. A bucket and a supply of mugs were placed next to it. The bucket and mugs were used when it was time to pass the Guinness around to the thirsty men. The farmer had to keep an eye on a few men to make sure they did not get an early start on the precious liquid!

Eventually, the threshing machine arrived drawn by a tractor. The owner of this threshing machine and tractor, was my uncle Mattie. The threshing machine was placed between the stacks of corn. Little holes were dug in the ground for the wheels of the threshing machine and tractor and the wheels were rolled into them. This was to keep the threshing machine and tractor steady during operation. A drive belt was attached from the tractor pulley wheel to the threshing machine pulley wheel. Placing the wheels of the tractor and threshing machine into the little holes in the ground, allowed the drive belt to be tight enough to rotate the pulley wheel of the threshing machine. Attaching the drive belt from the tractor to the threshing machine required great expertise because the pulley wheel of the tractor had to be perfectly lined up with the pulley wheel of the threshing machine. The drive belt had to be crossed because the pulley wheel of the tractor rotated in a clockwise direction, and the pulley wheel of the threshing machine had to rotate in a counter-clockwise direction.

When the threshing machine was set in motion, each man took up his position of work. Two men were on the stacks of sheaves passing them on to two men on top of the threshing machine, who fed them into the thresher to separate the grain from the straw. Two men were at the rear of the threshing machine attending to the grain pouring out into sacks. Several men with forks were removing straw which was streaming out from the front of the threshing machine. Several other men were taking this straw to where it was forked onto a very large stack. Another man was at one side of the threshing machine clearing away the chaff that was pouring out from underneath. The men with horse and carts were taking the sacks of grain to the barn for storage. My uncle Mattie was constantly checking the operating mechanism of the threshing machine, making sure that all belts were tight, and making sure that the machine was operating at the correct speed.

After a couple of hours of constant work, my father appeared with a bucket full of Guinness, which he drained from the barrel. The children brought along a supply of empty mugs. My father dipped empty mugs into the bucket of Guinness, which were passed around to the thirsty men. This called for a short break and time for a smoke and, of course, time to answer the call of nature! After this short break, work resumed until it was time to stop for dinner. Hungry men took their places around the many tables. Some of the tables were outside in the yard because there was no room for all of them inside. After the meal, they sat around for a little while for a chat and a smoke. Many of the men smoked pipes and had to go through the ritual of cutting the tobacco and filling their pipes. My uncle Mattie had gone out ahead of everyone to grease and lubricate the threshing machine and check the belts. In a short time, all the men were back at their positions and continued work for the afternoon. When the threshing was finished, another bucket of Guinness arrived. The cats had also arrived, looking for any mice which were hidden in the straw.

Some odds and ends had to be taken care of, such as raking down the large straw stack and raking up any loose straw on the ground. More Guinness was passed around until the barrel was completely empty. Arrangements were made for the location of the next day's threshing, and everyone promised to be there. My father thanked the men for their help with the customary words, "The Lord leave ye the health." Gradually the men left to go back to their own homes to milk their cows. Meanwhile, our own cows were already rounded up by the children who had brought them in for milking. Because my uncle Mattie lived with us, the threshing machine remained over night and was removed next morning to the next farmer on his list for threshing. My father followed on to help just as he was helped on the previous day. My mother also went along to help the woman of that house prepare to feed the hungry men at the threshing.

The days of the reaper and binder and threshing machine are long gone. They have been replaced by the combine harvester, which cuts the corn and threshes it at the same time with just a few men helping. The arrival of the combine harvester made my uncle Mattie's reaper and binder and threshing machine obsolete. The threshing machine, which was a "Garvey" model built in Aberdeen, Scotland, is now in a museum. The tractor, which was a 1935 Fordson, is now owned by a man who collects vintage tractors. Its engine is still in perfect operating condition. The registration number is HI 4278.

54

DANGEROUS MISCHIEF

MY UNCLE MATTIE WAS CONSTANTLY EXPLAINING TO ME THE internal mechanism of a threshing machine. I spent several hours with him when he was preparing the threshing machine for the threshing season. One afternoon, when he was about to set the threshing machine in motion, I got a dangerous idea into my head. While he was busy cranking up the tractor by turning a starting handle, I climbed into the lower part of the thresher where the chaff came out.

This part of the machine moves in a backward and forward direction to shake out the chaff. Overhead, there are other backward and forward moving parts. The upper and lower moving parts move in opposite directions from each other. There is very little space between both levels. Being small, I was able to fit in between them and lay flat. I did this because I wanted to get a thrill from the backward and forward movement of the chaff dispenser. My uncle Mattie did not know I was in there.

When he set the threshing machine in motion, the forward

and backward movement upset my stomach, making me puke up my guts. The chaff dispenser threw me out on the ground in the same way it threw out the chaff. When my uncle saw this happening, he immediately stopped the threshing machine. He got a terrible fright because I could have been mangled between the moving parts. I was so sick I thought I was going to die! My uncle got very upset. He grabbed me and gave me a stern lecture explaining how lucky I was that I did not get mangled in the moving parts. But I was so sick I was sort of wishing I did get killed! Then my father came on the scene and my uncle told him what had just happened. I got another lecture on the dangers of being inside a threshing machine when it is in operation. Then I realized what a foolish and dangerous mistake I made.

55

THE WREN BOYS

THE WREN HAS THE REPUTATION OF BEING THE KING OF ALL
birds. The story goes that there was a contest among the birds
to find out who could fly to the greatest heights. The eagle
soared higher than any other bird. However, a wren was
perched on the eagle's back. When the eagle got exhausted and
was unable to fly any higher, the wren took flight from the back
of the eagle and flew several feet higher. Because of this, it was
acclaimed as king of the birds.

Tradition holds that the wren by its chirping alerted the
Romans to where St. Stephen was hiding. St. Stephen was
captured and stoned to death as the first Christian martyr.
Other sources say that the wren caused the defeat of Irish
soldiers who were planning an attack on invading Norsemen,
who were sleeping. They were awakened by a wren pecking on
some breadcrumbs on a drum. For these and other reasons the
wren has been vilified. This led to the Irish custom of killing a
wren by stoning on St. Stephen's Day, which is December 26. In
time, this custom ended and was replaced by a reenactment.

The reenactment is placing an artificial wren on a holly bush on St. Stephen's Day. The holly bush is decorated with ribbons of various colors. Groups of people with an artificial wren on a decorated holly bush go from house to house. They dress in old tattered clothes, which are usually turned inside out. Some blacken their face with soot from the chimney. Others wear masks. At each house, they entertain the household with musical instruments and singing where they collect a small amount of money. The purpose of collecting money is to cover the funeral expense to bury the wren! The amount of money collected will vary depending on the quality of the entertainment provided. The most lucrative collections are when calling to a crowded public house. Some groups can be very good while others are useless. While going from door to door, the word wren is always pronounced as WRAN. On arrival at a house, the group recites the following rhyme:

The wran, the wran, the king of all birds,
St. Stephen's Day was caught in the furze.
Although he was little, his family was great.
Rise up N. _____ and give us a treat.

I followed this wran all day today,
Through muck and mire and yellow clay.
And brought him home on a holly tree.
This wran, this wran, that you may see,
A bunch of ribbons by his side.

Up with the kettle, and down with the pan,
And give us a penny to bury the wran.

Hunting the 'wran' as we called, it went on from early morning until late at night. It was helpful to be the early callers at a house. It was a great opportunity for young people to collect money. But going along the road in groups had its dangers. Sometimes one group would attack another group to rob them. This could lead to a fight, resulting in bloody noses. It was devastating for the group that was robbed, especially if the robbery took place late in the day when a substantial amount of money was collected. Sometimes individuals went alone. They were prime targets to be robbed. Sadly, in modern times, wren boys are seldom seen. Young people today have more money than those of previous generations.

56

THE PARISH MISSION

IT WAS CUSTOMARY IN IRELAND FOR PARISHES TO CONDUCT
an annual parish mission or retreat. It usually took place during
the month of May or the month of June. It went on from a
Sunday evening to the following Sunday evening. A missionary
priest from some religious order, typically a Redemptorist,
Passionist, Dominican, or Franciscan, was invited by the local
parish priest to visit the parish and preach a sermon each
evening. It was to be an occasion for spiritual renewal for the
parish. Mass was celebrated in the morning but not during the
evening service. The evening service began with the recitation
of the Rosary followed by a lengthy sermon, lasting at least
thirty minutes, and concluded with Benediction of the Blessed
Sacrament. On the final evening of the mission, it concluded
with the renewal of Baptismal promises. Stalls were erected
outside the church for the sale of religious articles such as
framed holy pictures, rosaries, medals, crucifixes, and holy
water fonts.

Before I left Ireland in 1967, the vast majority of people

attended church on a regular basis. During the week of the parish mission, everyone in the parish, with the exception of a few, attended. Every pew in the church was full as well as the gallery. There was standing room only at the entrances to the church. The very few, who were not attending, were known to everyone. Their names were mentioned in whispers! During the mission, the parish priest took the visiting missionary priest to make a house call to them. Somehow, everyone knew when that visit was made and what the outcome was! Because church attendance was considered very important for salvation, parishioners were concerned about the salvation of the few who did not attend.

My family home was on the boundary line of two parishes. The house and some fields were on one side of the line, and the majority of the fields were on the other side. This made us members of one parish and quasi members of the other parish. For this reason, my father always contributed to both parishes on a half and half basis. When the mission was held in each parish, we attended both of them. Somehow they were always held on different weeks. This was a great blessing to the children. It meant that cows were milked early on those evenings, and there was no additional field work after the evening meal. During the long daylight hours of summer, my father had us working in the fields until it got dark. The occasion of the parish mission gave us an excuse to get away from work and meet our friends after the mission while my father and his companions were having a few drinks in a public house. So we were fortunate to have had the opportunity to attend two parish missions instead of one!

There was a difference at each church. At one church I was an altar boy. All the altar boys attended. Because there were not enough seats in the sanctuary, some of us had to sit on the steps leading to the altar. Sometimes during the sermon, the missioner might get into a rage preaching about the torments of hell, and this amused us. Trying to control giggling was difficult when seated right under the nose of the missioner. There was no pulpit in that church, so the missioner preached from the top of the steps leading to the altar. This area is called the predella. When our giggling got out of control, the missioner stopped and looked down with a face that would frighten away the Devil. He might even pause and make a remark to the congregation about the bad behavior of the altar boys and complain about the conduct of modern day youth and encourage more discipline in the home.

Attending the mission at the other church was a little different. That church had a pulpit located some distance down the church. I was not an altar server at that church. On a few occasions, I went up into the gallery which was packed with people as well as the choir. One evening during the sermon, the missioner got into a rage and was shouting and bellowing about the evils of drink. My friends and I got into hysterics laughing and slapping each other on the shoulders. We considered it very funny. I noticed an older man watching us with dirty looks. He was well known to me and to my father. That night, when I got home after the mission, my father reprimanded me for my bad conduct in the church gallery. Right away I knew who told him! My father gave me strict orders never to set foot in that gallery again. Needless to say, I obeyed and did not go into that gallery until about sixty years later. That was on the occasion of my Golden Jubilee of ordination mass when I went up into the gallery to chat with the choir director about the music.

Because both churches did not have microphones or public

address systems, the missioner had to speak very loudly. It was amazing that they could be heard loud and clear anywhere in the church. They had powerful voices. When preaching, they put their heart and soul in what they were saying, and very often they worked up a sweat. Their sermons were what we refer to as hell fire and damnation. They certainly held the attention of everyone. The topics or subject matter of the sermons put the fear of God into the listeners. Typical topics were such matters as the evils of drink, gossip, company keeping, danger of riches, and what if you died suddenly that evening. Sweet Suffering Jesus, they could put the fear of God into the most hardened soul. This resulted in plenty of confessions. Sitting in the congregation, it was somewhat amusing to watch the reaction of the most hardened men, who had a reputation for drinking too much. They were squirming in their seats! When the topic was on company keeping, it was amusing to watch the reaction of young people, whose spirit was willing but their flesh was weak. When the topic was on gossip, it was a study to watch the faces of the women, who were well known for gossiping. A good or bad preacher was evaluated not so much on the content of his sermon, but on how much he shouted and got upset and frightened his listeners. The more he shouted and ranted and raved, the better preacher!

On the closing evening of the mission, there was the renewal of Baptism promises. Each person brought a candle to the mission. The candles were lighted during the Baptism promises, and after the mission they were donated to the church. During the renewal of Baptism promises, the missioner asked the congregation three questions to which they responded, "I do." If the response to the first question was not loud enough, the missioner asked for a louder response. At the closing of one particular mission, the missioner repeated the question asking if they renounced the world, the flesh, and the Devil. One man at the back of the church answered in a very loud voice, "I renounce the bastard."

At one parish, there was a local pipe band. After the closing of the mission in that parish, it was customary for the band to lead the missioner and the parish priest down the street from the church to the priest's house. With the mission over, the parish priest was happy that his parishioners had been spiritually renewed for another year and was hoping that the few, who did not attend church, were repentant and ready to return.

57

A WALL AND A FOOL

THE LOCAL PARISH PRIEST TOOK A DAILY WALK, FROM THE village out into the countryside. One Sunday afternoon while taking his customary walk he noticed a man working in a garden. A low stone wall separated the priest from the man in the garden. The priest reprimanded the man for working on the sabbath day. The man explained that he was digging potatoes for his dinner. The priest asked the man if the potatoes were good. The man responded that they were wonderful.

The priest then said to the man, "There is not much between you and a fool!"

The man replied to the priest, "Only the wall, Father!"

58

THE PRIEST AND THE CORNER BOY

THE PARISH PRIEST MENTIONED IN THE PREVIOUS STORY never drove a car. He went everywhere on his bicycle. One Monday morning, he was taking the money collected on the previous day to the bank in the next village, which was only a few miles away. As he cycled into the village where the bank was located, the parish priest of that village was standing at a street corner. He saw the other parish priest arriving on his bicycle with a bag of money hanging from the handlebars. As the priest on the bicycle passed by, the priest standing at the corner asked him, "Was the Sunday collection good?" The priest on the bicycle replied, "I don't discuss my business with corner boys!"

59

CHURCH COLLECTIONS

IN FORMER TIMES, PRIOR TO THE CURRENT PRACTICE OF taking up the Sunday collection during Mass, people on their way into church placed their contributions in a box located at the entrance to the church. There was usually a table at the entrance with two men guarding the money. At one church, the money was collected at an outdoor stand just inside the gate to the church grounds. The local parish priest usually stood near the stand with his walking stick watching people to see if they were putting money into the box. Whenever a person known to be poor put money in the box, he thanked them, and commented loudly on the generosity of the donor. But whenever a person known to be affluent passed by without making a contribution, he did not hesitate to sarcastically say out loud to the person, "I know you are a poor man. If you had money, you would give it." Because he said this loudly as people were passing by, it embarrassed the person who did not contribute. Very few went into the church without making a contribution.

That priest never retired and lived on to the age of ninety plus years. He was found dead in his chair one morning when he failed to show up for Mass. May he rest in peace.

60

SHARING A BULL

MY FATHER SHARED A HEREFORD BULL WITH TWO neighbors. He was a busy bull! The arrangement was that my father fed and housed the bull during the fall and winter months. The second neighbor kept the bull on his land for grazing during the spring and summer months. The third neighbor paid the insurance premium for the bull. The bull was sold after three or four years and replaced by another bull. It was always a Hereford white-faced bull that they purchased. Each bull had a different temperament. Bulls can never be trusted because they are very temperamental.

I have recollections of the different bulls we had. When walking a bull from one farm to another, one was on guard because the bull's temperament was subject to change. The bull had a rope threaded through the ring in his nose and up by its forehead and secured around the base of the horns. The movements of the bull were controlled by tugging on the rope in such a manner that the rope put pressure on the ring in his nose. When the bull was out grazing in a field, he was tied to a very long chain, which was anchored to the ground at one end by a spike. The other end of the chain was threaded through the ring on his nose and secured around the base of his horns. The reason a bull was chained was to keep him from servicing cows when the farmer was not watching. A farmer had to know when a cow was serviced to ensure that she was impregnated and to calculate the approximate due date of the birth of the calf.

In the winter months, the bull was housed in a cowhouse along with all the cows. Cows were tied up in stalls or bays. There were two cows to each bay. A feeding trough was at the head of each bay. The stalls and bays formed a long line with a slurry channel at the cow's rear end. A bull's torso was longer than a cow's torso. The bull shared a bay with a cow. But his longer torso placed his rear end further back than the cow's rear end. The bulls were generally smart about their toilet habits when they were housed in a cowhouse. Because their torso was longer than that of the cow next to them, whenever they were having a bowel movement, they nudged their rear end over against the cow and moved her sideways so that they could strategically place their rear end where the cow's rear end should be. When their bowel moved, they unloaded their pile! By doing this, when they lay down, the area behind them was clean. When the cow had to lie down, she had to tolerate the bull's droppings at her rear. This could be considered as sexual harassment of cows by bulls!

When the cows and the bull were in the cowhouse, the calves were in another house. When feeding time came for the calves, they were brought down to the cowhouse. Each calf went directly to its own mother and suckled from her udder. It was amazing how the calves recognized their own mothers.

While all cows and calves may look alike, there is a difference, which the farmer can detect. On one occasion when I was bringing the calves to their mothers for feeding, one calf got over excited. Instead to going to the udder of his mother, he went under the bull. He put his mouth up to where the cow's udder should be and put the bull's testicles into his mouth! The bull went crazy moaning and groaning in agony with his testicles in the mouth of the calf! The bull kicked the calf away while his testicles were still in the mouth of the calf. This caused a drag on the bull's testicles and increased his agony. The moaning and groaning from the bull was deafening! The calf eventually found his mother, and the bull was glad that he still had his jewels, even though they were hurting!

61

WORKING IN LONDON

IN THE SUMMER OF 1963, I WENT WITH A CLASSMATE TO work in London. Because I did not get any money for working at home on the farm during summer holidays, I decided to be financially independent by working in London. I was never outside of Ireland. This would be an adventure and a new experience for me. My classmate had arranged to stay with his brother, who was living in London. We were both assured of work on the buildings.

Shortly before departing for London, a man who was a native of our locality and a good friend of my father, was home on a holiday from London. When he heard that I was planning to work on the buildings, he did not think that was a good idea for me because I was going to be a priest. He was concerned that I would be exposed to the vulgar language of the workers. He did not realize that listening to vulgar language was nothing new to me, or that I was very fluent in that language! He persuaded me to stay with him and his wife in London, and that he would get me a nice clean job working with refined people.

After much persuasion from this man and from my father, I agreed to this. That turned out to be a bad mistake on my part!

My classmate and I took off for London on a Friday. We went by train to Rosslare Harbour, and from there by boat to Fishguard in Wales. Being out at sea and on a boat for the first time, I already felt like a world traveller! From Fishguard, we went by train to London. Arriving at Paddington Railway Station on a Saturday morning, we were met by my classmate's brother. Within minutes, we were going down an escalator and boarding an underground railway train. This really fascinated me. I had never heard of an underground railway system. By now, I felt I was a long way from Tipperary! We went to the home of my classmate's brother where we spent the weekend. On the Sunday evening, my classmate and his brother took me to the home of the man, who talked me into not taking a job on the buildings. Next morning, that man took me to my place of work and introduced me to the manager of the establishment. It was the Irish Club in Eaton Square.

The manager introduced me to the man that I would be working with. What a surprise I got. He was dressed in overalls and had a bucket and a mop with him. My father's friend had led me to believe that I was going to have some sort of a posh job working in an office. Because of this, I arrived for work in my black suit and tie with shoes polished. In a short time, I found myself cleaning toilets and mopping floors and polishing furniture, dressed in my best clothes. I thought to myself, *Surely, I can do better than this!* After my first day at work, I took the bus back to the house where I was staying. I told the man and his wife how disappointed I was with the type of work I had to do, and that there was no way I was going to settle for that. Their response made matters worse when they said that I had to start at the bottom and work my way up the ladder.

How could I do that in a few weeks? I had arranged with my classmate that I would join him the following weekend at his brother's house. I decided to stay at the Irish Club until the Friday, and then pack it in and get a job on the buildings. The man's wife with whom I was staying, worked as a salesperson at Selfridge's Department Store on Oxford Street near Marble Arch. When I came home from work the next day, she told me that she had a job for me at Selfridge's. They were willing to hire me because they were having a sale the following week and needed the extra staff. This made me feel that I was coming up in the world very fast. Within one week, I was going from cleaning toilets to being a salesman at a department store located in the very upper-class area of Oxford Street in London where only the very well-off can afford to shop. I agreed to accept this offer. I spent the weekend with my classmate and told him about my posh job at Selfridge's.

On the Monday morning, I found myself working as a sales-person in the linen department at Selfridge's. It did not take long for me to realize that this job was going to be another disaster. I was like a bull in a china shop, trying to cater to the very posh customers with very posh accents. To begin with, I did not understand a word they were saying with their cockney accents. When they asked for something, I did not know what I was looking for or where to find it. I was all thumbs and clumsy, trying to wrap packages and tie the twine around them. All the other staff around me were real whipper-snappers with a pencil over their ear and speaking with very posh accents. I had to act like I was very knowledgeable about the various brands of linens. This job was turning out to be a nightmare and more stressful than cleaning toilets at the Irish Club! I survived for a few days until disaster struck.

About my third day at work, a very intimidating posh woman approached me. She was dressed in a mink coat and was wearing a hat and gloves. She had a handbag hanging from her left arm. She was wearing lots and lots of jewelry. With a wave of her hand and a very domineering stance and attitude, she asked me if I would show her some Egyptian linen. I did not know such a brand of linen existed! But I had to show off my best display of confidence and knowledge about Egyptian linen. I invited the lady to follow me. I had no idea where I was going. After leading the woman up and down a few aisles, I spotted rolls of linen on a shelf. In my best Tipperary accent tainted with a little bit of a cockney accent, I pointed out a roll of linen, or what I thought was linen! I assured her that it was the best Egyptian linen she could find in the entire city of London. She removed her gloves and put the linen between her thumb and forefinger to feel it. Then acting very disgusted, she turned to me and said, "Young man, this is not Egyptian linen. It is just cheap cotton. I must speak to the manager at once!" I could not deal any longer with this. My temper got the best of me. I snapped at the woman and told her to find the ****** Egyptian linen herself!

I went straight to the business office before she got there to an announce my resignation and ask for my wages. My wages were very small because I was getting a base hourly pay plus commission. What I made on commission would hardly be enough to buy my bus ticket. The manager was extremely annoyed with me telling me that I was hired on the recommendation of a long time staff member and because of the upcoming sale. Without giving an explanation for resigning, I left the business office in a hurry before the intimidating woman arrived. I left the store and got on a bus to go home and wait for the man and his wife to come home and announce to them that I was going to work on the buildings. Needless to say, when they arrived home and got my news, they were very disappointed. I thanked them for their efforts to find work for me and for giving me a place to stay. Next morning, I got on an underground train and went on to the house of my classmate's brother. After a few days, he got me a job on the buildings.

I got a job as a chippy's mate. A chippy is a carpenter. My job was to assist a carpenter at his work. The location of my work was in the Blackwall Tunnel. This was a brand new motorway tunnel going under the River Thames. The entrance to the tunnel was located in the East End of London in the neighborhood associated with the serial killer, Jack the Ripper. I was satisfied with this job, and I was earning about three times more than at the two previous jobs.

I was working with two chippys or carpenters. One was an Englishman with a very cockney accent, and the other was an Irishman with a strong Kerry accent. The Irishman, being a cute Kerryman, was very curious to find out as much as he could about me. I never let it be known that I was a student for the priesthood, or that my employment there was to be temporary. I had planned to stay six weeks on the job before returning to Ireland and to college. So I was just another "Paddy" working in the tunnel. The chippys or carpenters I was working with were responsible for assembling the wood casings for the concrete to be poured. We were working in a very confined area. As the tunnel was being bored, I was fascinated by how the large drilling machine worked. Because we were boring a tunnel under the River Thames, I was a little concerned in case of a water leak from overhead.

Work began at eight o'clock in the morning. Around mid-morning we came up from the tunnel for a tea break in a wooden-framed hut, which served as a canteen at the entrance to the tunnel. We had to bring our own sandwich with us. The tea was provided in a large bucket into which everyone dipped their mugs to get their tea. The bucket of tea was delivered by a man who had no hands. He carried the bucket suspended by the handle from his lower arm. There was a hook at the end of both wrists. I was told that he lost both hands in an accident with a circular saw. I enjoyed my work in the tunnel. I had the opportunity to witness what was involved in boring a tunnel. It was a wonderful experience. Work ended each evening at five o'clock. The two carpenters headed for a local public house, and they always invited me to join them. I declined by telling them I had to go home to my wife and mind the children while she was working at night.

Going home from work I had to take Number 16 bus to Mile End underground railway station. From there I took the train to where I was staying. Getting on the train, I deliberately tried to sit near some of the typical London business men dressed in their pin striped three-piece suits and bowler hats with an umbrella dangling from the arm. I was wearing work clothes, stained with cement and looking like a common laborer. Taking my seat, they looked at me with disgust and tried to move away from me. Feeling liberated from my posh job at Selfridge's Department Store and the intimidating woman looking for Egyptian linen, I thought to myself that I might be earning more money than they were earning!

My classmate returned to Ireland two weeks ahead of me. I

stayed on the extra two weeks to make up for the miserable two weeks with small pay after arrival. For variety, I returned to Ireland by a different route. I took a train from Euston Railway Station to Hollyhead, and from there by boat to Dublin, and from there by train to Tipperary. It was my first experience of being a returned emigrant. It gave me an appreciation for the many Irish, who had to spend their life making a living outside of Ireland. I was delighted to inform my father that I heard very little, if any, vulgar language while working on the buildings!

62

ASH WEDNESDAY

On the morning of Ash Wednesday in rural Ireland, everyone could not attend morning Mass because of work. One person from each locality attended and received the Blessed Ashes on their forehead from the priest, who said, "Remember that you are dust, and to dust you will return." The ashes were from the burned palms of the Palm Sunday of the previous year. The person, who was representing each locality, brought home a container of the Blessed Ashes and placed them on the foreheads of everyone in that household. Someone from that house delivered the container of ashes to another house where someone in that household placed the ashes on the foreheads of all in that house.

The container of ashes was passed along from one household to another household until each home had received the ashes. Finally, the ashes were delivered to the local school where the teachers placed the ashes on the forehead of each pupil. It was a distinct honor for the pupil chosen to place the ashes on the teacher's forehead! There were always a few pupils who were hoping that the ashes placed on the teacher's forehead might be hot! After everyone had received the ashes on their foreheads, the remaining ashes were thrown into the fire.

63

EASTER WATER AND PISHOGUES

DURING THE EASTER VIGIL MASS, WATER IN THE BAPTISM font was blessed. In rural Irish churches, not only was water in the baptism font blessed, but gallons of water in other containers were also blessed. The containers were a few twenty gallon milk churns borrowed from local farmers. After the Easter Vigil Mass and after the Masses on Easter Sunday morning, parishioners dipped containers in to the milk churns and filled them up with Easter Water. The containers were usually one pint whiskey bottles, beer bottles, and sometimes kettles or empty paint cans. The containers full of Holy Water were taken home and clearly labelled Easter Water. This water was always kept in a separate place from regular Holy Water. It was considered to be very powerful for driving away the Devil. On Easter Sunday morning in my home, it was customary for each of us in turn to go outside then come in and wish everyone a Happy Easter. After doing this, we had to take three sips of Easter Water while saying, "In the name of the Father, and of the Son, and of the Holy Ghost."

A generous supply of Easter Water was sprinkled on all the cattle and other livestock in the sheds and fields on the evening of the last day of April, known as May Eve. It was believed that on this evening evil spirits were at work. These evil spirits were known as "Pishogues." Before the arrival of Christianity in Ireland, the pagan Irish worshipped the Sun God, or the God of Fire. The Gaelic name is "Bealtinne," which translates as the month of May. There were some individuals in every locality, who had a reputation as being agents of the Devil and were to be avoided. They were referred to as being "Street Angels and House Devils." Such individuals were very unwelcome in any house or farmyard on May Eve. There was a person in my locality, who had this reputation. Whenever this person called to our house, when leaving, Holy Water from the little holy water font by the door was sprinkled on that person's heels.

On May Eve, it was considered to be bad luck to loan anything or give anything away on that day. By doing So that item would be scarce during the coming year. We had a water pump in our yard. On May Eve, the handle of the pump was tied up by a lock and chain so that nobody could draw water from it. Finding an egg placed in some unusual place on May Eve was a sign that someone placed it there to wish bad luck. Some people really believed this and stayed awake all night watching their property. They got very upset if they found an egg in some place where there was no way a hen could have laid it. Pranksters in the locality were known to deliberately place eggs somewhere on the property of those nervous people!

Back then, rural Irish people were deeply religious, but they had many superstitious beliefs. The vast majority of them had received only a primary school education. But in spite of this, they were very intelligent, and possessed plenty of common sense. They were very wise and shrewd in managing and conducting their business. But very few of them had the opportunity to travel far from their native locality. Those days are long gone, and rural Irish people today are very learned and sophisticated and have travelled to far away places.

64

PLOUGHING IN MONTANA

WHEN JACK FITZGERALD WAS A VERY YOUNG MAN, HE SPENT a few years working in the state of Montana close to the border of Canada. This was in the 1930s. He went there for an adventure and to see what life was like in far away places. Montana is known as "Big Sky Country." While in Montana, he spent some time working for a farmer ploughing fields with a pair of horses pulling the plough.

When he returned to Ireland, he had plenty of stories for the locals. However, they found some of his stories hard to believe. One of his stories was about ploughing a field in Montana with a pair of horses. He claimed that there was approximately one hundred acres in the field. He told that the field was so long that when he set off in the morning from the headland, he would be lucky to be back in time for his dinner in the evening. The locals did not believe this.

Some years ago, I was visiting a classmate in Mankato, Minnesota. Minnesota is similar to Montana in that is another of the large states west of the Mississippi River with farm properties expanding for several miles. My classmate had a parishioner, who was a farmer. He grew about a thousand acres of soybeans. One day I had the opportunity to see a soybean harvester at work, and I took a spin on it. Starting out from the headland, I could not see any fence in the distance. As we moved along, I discovered that what I was seeing from the headland was only the horizon on the brow of a hill. When we got to the brow of the hill, the distance ahead to the opposite headland was nearly twice as long as the distance we had travelled from the starting headland. It took us almost one hour to arrive back to where we started. Considering that a soybean harvester was moving much faster than Jack Fitzgerald's two horses pulling a plough, I was convinced then that Jack Fitzgerald's story was credible!

65

THE SKYSCRAPER AND THE MOON

ANOTHER ONE OF JACK FITZGERALD'S STORIES FROM AMERICA was about the skyscraper and the moon. He was trying to explain to the locals what a skyscraper looked like. He said they were so high that there was no way one could look up to the top of them while standing upright. A person's neck was not flexible enough to do this. He said that the only way to look all the way to the top of a skyscraper was to lie on one's back on the ground and look up.

He went on to say that there was a problem with one skyscraper. When it was completed, it was so high that the moon could not pass over it! Workers had to go up and remove several layers of bricks to allow the moon to pass over it! Needless to say, the locals did not believe this story, but it gave them a great laugh!

66

STUDY FOR PRIESTHOOD

WHEN I FINISHED SECONDARY SCHOOL IN JUNE 1961, I WAS
very anxious to study to become a veterinary surgeon or some
profession connected with agriculture. But I also had considered the priesthood. It seems to be that during that period in
Ireland, every boy gave some consideration to being a priest.
We were constantly listening to priests from foreign countries
talking about the need for priests in those far away places. At
that time, Ireland had an abundance of priests, and only a
limited number of students were accepted to study to become
priests in Ireland.

To add to my troubles in making a decision, I also had
received an agricultural scholarship. To pursue veterinary or
priesthood would result in declining the scholarship. After
much consideration and consultation with a veterinary surgeon
in Tipperary town and with a few priests, I decided to try the
priesthood first. By doing this I would know after one or two
years if that was what I should pursue. If I dropped out, then I
could take up veterinary study.

Because I had spent five years in boarding school at St. Peter's College in Wexford and because there was a seminary attached to the college, I decided to enroll there. There were five others from my class in the secondary school, who were entering St. Peter's, as well as many others in classes ahead of me, who were already there. This influenced my decision to go there. I had also considered going to St. Columban's College in Dalgan Park, Navan, County Meath to join the Columban Fathers. Their missions were mainly in the Far East. I decided against that because I would have to learn a foreign language, and I would get back to Ireland for a holiday only every seven years. This left St. Peter's in Wexford as my choice.

Before going to the seminary, I had to get a black suit of clothes, a black hat, and a soutane or cassock. My father took me to Limerick City to be fitted for the clothing. The store was Beecher's on O'Connell Street. While the clerk was taking my measurements, my father kept distracting him by complaining about the fact that he considered it a waste of time and a waste of money getting me a black suit. He predicted that I would drop out by Christmas. Because he would not stop talking, the clerk had to beg him to stop because he was unable to concentrate on my measurements due to my father's constant complaining. To make a long story short, I got all the clothing I needed, and I was on my way to the seminary in early September 1961.

The journey was by train from Limerick Junction to Wexford. The train fare was thirty shillings one way. Because I had very little money, I saw an opportunity here to get some cash on this. Each time my father took me to the train station, I had him keep an eye on my baggage while I went to the ticket office. I got a one-way ticket to the next station, which was a very short distance away in Tipperary town. This ticket cost only nine pence. This meant that I had twenty-nine shillings and three pence to put into my pocket. On arrival in Tipperary, town I got off the train and hitched a ride all the way to Wexford. When it came time to come home for holidays, I got the train fare of thirty shillings from home. I hitched a ride from Wexford to Tipperary town. Then I took the train the short distance to Limerick Junction at a cost of nine pence. So I had another twenty-nine shillings and three pence in my pocket. Not knowing how long it would take me to hitch a ride from Wexford to Tipperary, I gave myself plenty of time by letting them know at home that I would arrive at Limerick Junction on the last train. My father was always there to meet me thinking I came the entire journey by train!

Because I had spent the previous five years in the secondary school at St. Peter's, the President of the Seminary informed me that I was eligible to study for the local Diocese of Ferns. But being interested in going to some place where priests were needed, I declined the offer. Sometimes I regret that decision. I would have been very happy as a priest in Ireland. At the beginning of my study for the priesthood, there were twenty-five in my class. By the time of ordination six years later, we had seventeen. During that first year, we had priests from different dioceses throughout the world visit the seminary looking for students to come and work in their diocese. After listening to them, I narrowed it down to San Antonio, Texas; San Diego, California; or Savannah, Georgia. I opted to study for the Diocese of Savannah. I was influenced by the fact that I had learned that many of the people in Savannah had Wexford origins. During my six years in the seminary, there were a few times I had serious doubts and considered dropping out. But I

153

persevered and was ordained on June 4, 1967. However, my time in seminary was not without some troubles. I had a tendency to be in the wrong place at the wrong time! Just as I was about to enter my final year, disaster struck! I was almost expelled! What happened?

My bedroom was on the same floor as the Dean's bedroom. He had a very comfortable room with a bathroom attached, complete with a nice bathtub. Students had to settle for a common toilet area. The shower stalls were located in a separate area. Showers were taken in order of seniority with very limited time to take a shower. There was always the possibility of the water going cold during the time allotted for taking showers. The Dean was away for one week. During that time, his bathtub was not in use and his room door was not locked. I decided to make use of his bathtub. That was the worst decision I ever made!

I went to the Dean's room and filled up the bathtub and got into it. It felt so good! After about five minutes soaking in the bathtub, the Dean arrived in the room. He got sick while away and returned unexpectedly. He got a terrible fright when he saw me in the bathtub, and I was speechless. When he regained his speech, he asked me why was I using his bathtub. I was unable to respond. He ordered me to get out of the bathtub and report back to him in twenty minutes. He left the room very angry and slammed his bedroom door so hard that the entire room vibrated. When I returned to his room, he gave me a lecture that I will never forget and informed me that I would have to appear before a panel of professors, who would decide on an appropriate punishment, which more than likely would be expulsion. That night I did not sleep and regretted that I did not study to be a veterinary surgeon. I kept thinking about my father's prediction when I was getting my black suit. He was right!

Next day, I appeared before a panel of five priest professors. The panel consisted of the President, the Vice President, the Dean, and two other priests. The President spoke about the seriousness of my crime and indicated that I was not a suitable candidate for Holy Orders. I was judged as a criminal and deserved expulsion. Each priest gave his opinion on the matter. I sat there in silence like a puppy dog being scolded. After everyone had made their comments, the President called for a vote. The vote was to determine whether I should be expelled or placed on probation. The President asked those in favor of expulsion to raise their hand. Two priests raised their hand. That left three hands in favor of probation. That was a relief! I was given a stern warning by the President. He concluded by saying to me, "Should you decide not to return after the summer holidays, you will be as free as a bird." How encouraging! I was then dismissed. At that moment, I was determined to be a priest. I spent my final year being an exemplary student.

About one year after that encounter with the panel of priests, I was ordained. Following the ordination ceremony, it was customary for the newly ordained to give his priestly blessing to his professors. That morning, the two priests, who voted to have me expelled, knelt for my blessing and congratulated me and wished me well. As the years went by after ordination, whenever I returned to visit, I always received a very warm welcome and was referred to as the stone rejected by the builders!

67

MY ORDINATION

I WAS ORDAINED TO THE PRIESTHOOD ON THE MORNING OF Sunday, June 4, 1967 by Bishop Donal Herlihy, who was the Bishop of the local Diocese of Ferns. The ordination took place in the college chapel. There were seventeen in my class. One was ordained two weeks earlier in his native Wales by his own bishop. Another classmate's ordination was delayed for a few months because he had not reached the required minimum age for ordination. Fifteen of us were ordained that morning in the college chapel. Because of limited seating in the chapel, we were allowed to invite fifteen guests each. My guests were my parents, brothers, sister, aunts, uncles, and a few close family friends. Those with very large families had the challenge of who to select as guests. A few of the candidates for ordination had small families. If they had spare tickets, they gladly shared them with those who needed more.

My family arrived in Wexford on the evening prior to the ordination. I had accommodations arranged for them at White's Hotel in Wexford town. My father and mother and sister stayed with Sheila O'Connor, who was the owner of The Star Restaurant in the town. We developed a close friendship with her during my years in Wexford. It began in 1956 when my father and cousin first took me to Wexford to have me locked up in the boarding school! On that day in 1956, my father and cousin were looking for a place to eat. They ate at the Star Restaurant, and that was the beginning of our friendship with Sheila O'Connor. I was allowed a brief visit with my family on the evening before ordination. I will always remember my father taking me aside at the end of that meeting and asking me, "Are you sure you want to be a priest? It is still not too late to change your mind."

On the morning of ordination, my family took their seats in the chapel. The seats in the chapel were arranged lengthwise down the chapel facing the seats on the opposite side of the center aisle. This arrangement was for choir purposes. I am sure they found this seating arrangement strange! Families were seated according to the order of seniority of the person to be ordained. I was fourth in seniority in my class, so my family was seated close to the altar. Immediately following the ceremony, we went outside and were joined by our families to impart an individual blessing on each one of them. My first blessing was to my mother, followed by my father, and then to my brothers and sister and other invited guests. After this, the newly ordained were treated to breakfast in the dining room of the professors. This was the very first time we saw the inside of that room! On the way into the room, the professors were kneeling at the door for a blessing from each one of us. I found this to be a very humbling experience, especially when imparting my blessing on the two professors, who had voted to have me expelled just one year previously! The professors joined us at the very large table for breakfast. We were no longer students and professors. We were all equal!

After breakfast we had a group photograph taken. By now, everyone attending the ordination had assembled in one area to receive individual blessings. Over the years, some of us had come to know each others families. This added to the joy of the moment imparting blessings on the families of classmates. After this, we all went our separate ways to various hotels and restaurants in the town for lunch. But before doing So we bid farewell to each other. It would be the last time we were together as a group. In a few weeks, we would be working in various parts of the world. Some were staying in Ireland. Others were going to England, Scotland, Wales, America, and Australia.

68

MY FIRST MASS

On Monday, June 5, 1967, which was the day following my ordination, I celebrated my first Mass. It was at my local parish church of St. Nicholas at Solohead near Tipperary town. The time was 10:30 in the morning. This time was selected because it allowed the local farmers to attend after they had delivered their milk to the creamery. I can vividly recall the large number of horses and carts, donkeys and carts, tractors and trailers, around the area near the church. I can recall one horse and cart tied to the cemetery gate and a donkey and cart tied to the spokes of the wheel of the horse's cart. Horses and carts and donkeys and carts were also tied to trees along the roadside. As well as this, there were motor cars parked everywhere. The church was packed to capacity and overflowing out into the church grounds.

At that time, Mass was celebrated on the old high altar facing the wall. The priest had his back toward the congregation. This was shortly after the Second Vatican Council. Parts of the Mass were still in Latin and other parts were in English.

People knelt at the altar railing to receive Holy Communion. My altar server was Dick Browne, who later went to study for the priesthood, and is now the Parish Priest in Cappamore. Because it was my First Mass, I had a priest standing next to me to help me in case I got flustered. That priest was Father Owen O'Neill, who was ordained two years previously for the Diocese of Nottingham in England. There were several other priests seated in the sanctuary. We did not have concelebrated Masses at that time, so they were dressed in soutane (cassock) and surplice. Among them was the local Parish Priest, Father Michael English, who attended my ordination on the previous day.

All went well until the distribution of Holy Communion. Even though there were several other priests present, they did not help with the distribution of Holy Communion. The newly ordained priest distributed Holy Communion on his own. This was because people wanted to receive from the newly ordained priest. People came forward and knelt at the altar railing to receive. Having distributed Holy Communion to a multitude of people, I needed more Sacred Hosts. I went to the Tabernacle expecting to find more. To my horror, I found the Tabernacle empty! Father English came to me to confirm that we had run out of Sacred Hosts. In my estimation, about half of those attending the Mass were deprived of receiving Holy Communion. Afterwards, Father English explained that he underestimated the number of people he was expecting to receive. At that time, people did not receive Holy Communion as frequently as they do now. The reason for the unusually large number receiving on that day was because the annual parish mission concluded the previous evening. Everyone was spiritually renewed and properly disposed to receive! At the conclusion of Mass, everyone got in line to find a place to kneel at the altar rail to receive my blessing. With so many people to individually bless, this took about one hour. After this, my family, relatives, and friends went to a hotel in Tipperary town for a meal. The hotel was then named Hotel Tipperary. It was previously named Dobbyns Hotel and is now named Times Square. After the meal, there were speeches given by various people, which included some of my former teachers from Primary and Secondary School. After the speeches, there was music and dancing for several hours.

On the following day, Tuesday, June 6, 1967, I celebrated Mass at Cappawhite Church, which was our quasi parish and where I served Mass as an altar boy. On the next day, Wednesday, June 7, 1967, I celebrated Mass at Donohill Church, which was my mother's childhood church and where my father and mother were married. Before going to America on August 25, 1967, I was allowed to celebrate three Masses at my home, and one Mass at the house of an uncle or aunt. Primary Schools did not close for summer holidays until early July so I was able to visit my local school at Ayle and the Christian Brothers school in Tipperary town. I also visited the homes of local families. The most memorable home I visited to give my blessing was to the home of Mrs. Winnie McGrath. That was the house with the lovely yellow ochre walls at which I threw a fistful of wet mud for which I was severely punished. Winnie McGrath got down on her feeble old knees for my blessing and reminded me of the wet mud I threw at her wall and told me that I was a bold boy when I was growing up, but I turned out good!

69

MY FIRST EMERGENCY CALL

SEVERAL WEEKS AFTER MY ORDINATION, THE TWO PRIESTS AT my parish church were away for one week. They arranged with me to take care of the weekday Mass and sick calls. I was glad to have the opportunity to do temporary full-time ministry. I agreed to take up residence in the Parochial House during that week. It was a very large house. I was given a bedroom, which was reserved for the Archbishop whenever he visited the parish. The room had a very large bed with an ornate brass headboard. I felt very important sleeping in the Archbishop's bed! There was just one telephone in the house, which was located at the bottom of the stairs. This was not unusual at that time. Most homes did not even have a telephone. We did not have a phone in my home, and so I was not used to hearing a telephone ring.

A short distance away was Limerick Junction railway station. On Saturday, July 29, 1967, at 2:30 in the morning, a southbound freight train from Dublin to Cork was pulling out from the station platform and was crossing over several tracks to the rail line for Cork. At that very time, a non-stop north-bound freight train from Cork to Dublin approached the station at great speed. It crashed into the train, which was crossing the tracks. Assuming that the locomotive driver of the Dublin bound train was killed, a phone call was made to the Parochial House where I was sound asleep. I did not hear the phone ringing because my room door was closed and the phone was located all the way down to the bottom of the stairs.

When morning came, as I was making my way to the church for Mass, I was informed about the horrible train crash during the night at Limerick Junction railway station. At this time, I did not know that it was two freight trains that were involved. I was thinking if there was a passenger train involved, I would surely have got a phone call. Not having heard any phone ringing, I concluded that a passenger train was not involved and perhaps the crash was not as serious as was being reported to me. After Mass, I drove to the railway station to investigate. On arrival, I saw train wagons piled high on top of each other and wheels and wreckage strewn everywhere. It was a dreadful sight. There was an eerie silence, except for moans coming from cattle, who were seriously injured in the crash. I entered the railway station and met the Station Master. He was angry and complained that he phoned the Parochial House looking for a priest and was upset over the fact the two priests did not answer the phone! He went on to say that he got one of the priests in Tipperary town to answer the phone and come out to the station. To save the good reputation of the two priests, I confessed that they were away, and that I was the priest on duty. It was a humiliating moment for me. I apolo-gized for not hearing the phone and became very conscious of the fact that I had missed my first emergency call. But I tried to stay positive by rationalizing that perhaps it was best that I did not get that call because it would have been a very dramatic experience for a newly ordained priest. Maybe God wanted an older and more experienced priest to deal with that situation.

When they went through the wreckage to get to the locomotive driver, they were surprised to find that he was not killed. How he escaped death was a miracle! About fifty cattle were killed. Veterinary surgeons were on hand to put down the seriously injured cattle. There were also several brand new cars on the train, which were damaged.

That train accident happened during the early hours of a Saturday morning, which was my last day on duty. The two priests returned that day, and I was relieved from my parish duties. I made sure to tell them about how I missed the emergency call to the train crash at Limerick Junction. It was better that they heard it from me instead of from the Station Master. They were very understanding but remarked that maybe I was too comfortable sleeping in the Archbishop's bed!

70

MY FAREWELL PARTY

ON THE NIGHT OF THURSDAY, AUGUST 24, 1967, WHICH WAS
the night before my departure for America, we had a farewell
party at my home. Family, relatives, neighbors, and friends
attended. There was plenty of music, singing, and dancing.
Everyone had a good time, but there was some sadness. The
older people at that time considered that going to America
meant never returning. They recalled past times when some
members of their families left for America and never returned.
But times had changed, and the world was getting smaller.
Travel to and from America was no longer by ship which took
several days. The "jet age" had arrived, and it took only the
same number of hours, as it as it did days in previous times, to
cross the Atlantic Ocean. My uncle Danny O'Neill left Ireland
for America in 1930 by ship and had never returned. The
farewell parties for a person going to America back then were
referred to as "The American Wake." But those tearful days
were long gone, and I assured everyone that I would return the

following summer. This I did, and I brought my uncle Danny
O'Neill home with me!

71

DEPARTURE FOR AMERICA

ON THE MORNING OF FRIDAY, AUGUST 25, 1967, I LEFT MY
home for Shannon Airport. Even though I was going to return
the following summer, it was a heartbreaking and very tearful
experience. Several people came to see me off. It was a new
experience for me checking baggage and making sure I had my
passport and immigration documents. As I bid farewell to
board the plane, everyone was crying, and I was crying. I joined
the procession of passengers making their way to the plane. At
that time, we had to walk out to the plane. I looked up at the
people on the observation deck. I clearly saw my father waving
his hat with one hand and with a handkerchief in his other
hand. I saw my mother holding a handkerchief to her eyes.
When I got to the top of the stairs, I turned around and waved
good-bye and entered the plane. It was a Boeing 707 Aer
Linguus Flight 104 for Kennedy Airport in New York. Shortly
after that, the plane pulled out from the terminal to prepare for
take-off. Within minutes, we were in the air and on our way to
the shores of America.

PART II
STORIES FROM AMERICA

72

ARRIVAL IN AMERICA

I WAS ORDAINED ON JUNE 4, 1967, AT ST. PETER'S COLLEGE in Wexford, Ireland. I left Ireland from Shannon Airport for America on a Boeing 707 Aer Lingus plane on August 25, 1967. I had a classmate traveling with me. It was a very emotional departure. Back then, going to America was seen as going to a very far away place, and there would be many changes before one would return. I was going one week ahead of my scheduled arrival in Savannah because I wanted to spend some time in New York with my uncle Daniel O'Neill, who I had never met. He left Ireland on February 22, 1930, and never returned. He went to America by ship, which took him seven days. I was traveling by air, which would take seven hours. It was my first time on a plane. We boarded by walking out to the plane and up the external stairwell to the plane. At the top of the steps before entering the plane, I stood and turned around and waved back at the crowds on the observation deck. I could clearly see my father waving his hat and my mother with a handkerchief to her eyes. I thought my heart would break as I entered the plane with tears streaming down my face. If there was ever a time I regretted becoming a priest for ministry in a foreign land, it was at that time.

I was seated next to a judge from Kansas City. On the journey over, he showed me how to count American coins. I could not understand why a nickel had less value than a dime, which was smaller in size. He gave me his address. I did not understand the purpose of the zip code in his address since we did not have postcodes or zip codes on Irish addresses.

On arriving at Kennedy Airport, I was amazed at the size of the place and all the planes on the ground compared to the size of Shannon Airport. We deplaned by walking down the external stairwell. I was directed through immigration where I was interrogated by a very unfriendly immigration officer. Because I was arriving, not as a visitor, but as one seeking permanent residence, I had to produce documentation, which the immigration officer scrutinized before stamping my passport and in a grumpy voice said, "Welcome to America." Having never before travelled by plane, finding out how to collect my bags was a new experience. I was fascinated by the conveyor belt, which delivered the bags. While going through immigration and customs, I could not understand why I was perspiring so much. I was extremely uncomfortable. Later I found out this was because of the heat and humidity.

After collecting my bags, my classmate and I proceeded to the arrivals hall. We were to be met by my uncle, who I had never met and by a cousin, Tom Chambers, who I had met in Ireland many times. When we reached the arrivals hall, I saw Tom Chambers, and he introduced me to my uncle, Danny O'Neill. I was very surprised to find that my uncle Danny, who had been in America for thirty-seven years had never lost his

Tipperary accent! He was asking me so many questions about his brothers and sisters back home, and he was not giving me time to answer before he asked the next question. We went to the parking lot, which was massive compared to the parking lot at Shannon Airport. Tom Chambers drove us into Brooklyn— driving on the wrong side of the road. On arrival at my uncle's house, I met his family, my first cousins, for the first time. My uncle decided that we should send a telegram to my family in Ireland to let them know that I had arrived safely. We did not have a telephone at home. So sending a telegram was the only way to send a message. Because of the time difference, I went to bed after eating. It was so hot in the house that the only bed covering I had was a sheet.

The following day, which was a Saturday, Tom Chambers and a friend drove us to Atlantic City, New Jersey. On the way, I noticed that the driver never changed gears and that the car did not have a clutch. I asked about this and discovered that cars in America had automatic transmission. When we arrived in Atlantic City, we took a walk along the boardwalk. Tom asked me if I would like to eat a hotdog. I was shocked that he would ask me if I would eat a dog. After he explained what a hotdog was, I agreed to try one. So I eat my first American hotdog on the boardwalk in Atlantic City. On the way back to New York, we stopped to get petrol or gasoline as they call it here. I noticed that the car did not have any headlights. When I asked about this, a switch was flopped and the hidden headlights rolled out. I remarked to my cousin that if he was thinking like an Irish person, he would have told me that this was his daytime car and that I should wait until I see the headlights of his nighttime car!

The following day was a Sunday, so I concelebrated Mass at

Our Lady of Angels Church in Brooklyn with Bishop Board-man, who was the Auxiliary Bishop of Brooklyn, and who resided at that church. It was my first time concelebrating Mass and also my first time celebrating Mass facing the people. This was shortly after Vatican Council II and Mass in my home parish in Ireland was still celebrated with the priest's back to the people with the altar facing the wall.

We remained in Brooklyn, New York, until the following Friday before going on to Savannah. During our time in New York, my uncle and my cousin showed me the many sites, including a visit to the United Nations Headquarters and going up to the top of the 108 story high Empire State Building. During my week in New York, I noticed that many of the windows in many of the houses had what appeared to be bird-cages. I remarked that the Americans must be very fond of having pet birds in their homes. I was informed that they were not bird cages but air condition units.

73

SAVANNAH, GEORGIA

On Friday, September 1, 1967, at Kennedy Airport, nine other newly ordained priests from Ireland joined me as we boarded a National Airlines propeller plane for a flight to Savannah, Georgia. On arrival in Savannah, the Bishop of Savannah and several local priests met us at the bottom of the steps from the plane. It was about nine in the evening, and the heat and humidity was very bad. Cars took us to various churches where we would stay for the weekend until we received out parish assignments. On Monday morning, September 4, 1967, all ten newly ordained Irish priests met with the Bishop in his office. I, along with four others, was assigned to study at The Pastoral Institute in New Orleans. This was to be a six-month orientation program to introduce us to various pastoral programs. At the end of the six-month period, we would return to Savannah and the other five priests would go to New Orleans to participate in this program. After our meeting with the bishop, he took us to lunch at The Pirate's House. When the waitress asked us if we wanted tea or coffee, all us being straight from Ireland, indicated that we wanted tea. The waitress then brought out several glasses filled with what looked like Coke. Thinking it was a Coke, I took a good sip and got a terrible shock at the taste. It was iced tea. It was terrible. We learned that in this part of America, when you ask for tea, you get only iced tea. If you want hot tea, you must specify that you want HOT tea. Eventually iced tea became one of my favorite drinks!

I had a week in Savannah before going to New Orleans. The first item of business for me was to get a new suit of clothes. Because it was so hot and humid, I had to get out of my heavy serge Irish suit. I purchased a lightweight suit for sixty dollars. I arrived in America with about one hundred and fifty dollars in my pocket. The purchase of the suit left me with only ninety dollars to my name in a foreign country. I was a poor immigrant. During that time, I did a driving test to obtain a Georgia Driving License. I was based at St. James Church in Savannah. Before taking the driving test, I drove around the school building a few times to get used to driving on the left hand side and to get used to operating an automatic transmission and power steering. When I went for the driving test, I had to drive through a long line of barrels and reverse back through them without knocking any of them over. After this, came the road test. I was delighted that I passed.

74

NEW ORLEANS, LOUISANA

THE BISHOP OF SAVANNAH, GERALD L. FREY, DROVE FIVE OF us Irish priests from Savannah to New Orleans. It was a six-hundred-mile journey. We left Savannah in the morning and arrived in New Orleans in the evening. Along the way, we stopped at Tallahassee, Florida; Mobile, Alabama; and Biloxi, Mississippi. We spent the night at Notre Dame Seminary. During our time in New Orleans, each of us was in residence in a parish. I was at St. Anthony Church in Gretna, which is a suburb of New Orleans located across the Mississippi River. The pastor of the parish, Father Gerard W. Poche, took me there. He was a native of New Orleans. Driving across the bridge over the mighty Mississippi River, I was amazed at the vast expanse of the river. As I took in the view of the river, Father Poche casually informed me that as soon as he dropped me off at the church that he was leaving for a wedding in Baton Rouge and would be back late that night. Then he informed me that there was a wedding scheduled at the church that after-noon, and that I would have to officiate. When I informed him that I had never officiated at a wedding, he replied that he would give me a quick run through the ceremony. This was a parish with over two thousand families, and he was the only priest there so I had no choice but to do it. There was a very elderly retired ninety-year-old priest in the parish by the name of Father Xavier Roumbouts, who was a native of Holland. He came to America in 1912. He still had a very strong Dutch accent. When I asked him when his last visit home to Holland was, he replied that he had never gone back there. After getting a crash lesson from Father Poche on how to officiate at a wedding, he took off, and on his way out the door, he informed me that I had to take the evening confessions.

On my first Sunday afternoon while walking in a park, I saw a very high embankment. My curiosity made me find out what was at the other side of the embankment. I climbed up to the top of it and discovered that it was holding back the mighty Mississippi River. Because the city of New Orleans is ten feet below sea level there are embankments or levees to keep the water out. Looking at the Mississippi River and the embankment, I thought of the poem I had learned back in school about little Hans the Dutch boy, who stuck his finger in the Zinder Zee.

The program in New Orleans involved hospital visitation, prison visitation, working at a slum parish one day a week, teaching in a high school, and being a part-time assistant (curate) at the parish where I was in residence. The people were very friendly and being an Irish priest with an Irish accent, I became somewhat of a novelty for them. Most of the people there are of French background with a mall mixture of Irish. The Irish settled there to help build the canals.

I became very friendly with a few families. They invited me

to their home for dinner. Sometimes they took me out to a restaurant in the city. One night I was taken to a restaurant, which was located on the very top floor of a very tall building. The room was circular, and it had a slowly revolving floor, which gave one a chance to look out over different parts the city while eating. I did not know that the floor was moving when I sat at a table by a window. My friends asked me if I would like a beer or something to drink. At that time in my life I was not drinking alcohol, but I decided to have a beer. A little while later I got the feeling that the floor was moving, and I was wondering if the beer was doing this. I did not want my friends to think I was drunk by asking if the floor was moving. But after about fifteen minutes, I was convinced that the floor had to be moving because looking out the window the view was constantly changing. So I asked if the floor was moving. I was relieved to know that I was not drunk, and that the floor was actually moving.

After six months in New Orleans, it was time to return to the Diocese of Savannah. I had grown attached to the city and the friends I had mad made there. I consider New Orleans as my first home in America. All five of us Irish priests drove back to Georgia, taking turns at driving along the way. When it was my turn to drive, it was from Mobile to Montgomery in Alabama. This was an Interstate motorway. The car was a typical very large American car of that era. I wanted to see how fast it could really go. I got up to a speed of 90 miles per hour without realizing that I had overtaken a police car. The police car chased me with blue lights flashing and siren blaring. I pulled over, and the police officer reprimanded me for such excessive speed. The Interstate Highway was number 85 and it had this number posted in various locations along the way. I pulled a fast one on the police officer by telling him that I was new in the country, and that I thought that the signs along the road showing 85, was actually the speed limit! He actually believed me and explained to me that this was the road number and not the speed limit sign. He cautioned me to observe the speed limit and drive safely in America.

75

DRIVE IN MOVIE THEATRES

IN A PREVIOUS STORY I WROTE ABOUT TAKING A GOAT TO A movie cinema in Ireland. Going to the movies in America was a new experience. The first movie film I went to see in America was at Radio City in New York. The title of the movie was *Guess Who Is Coming to Dinner* starring Sidney Poitier. The movie screen and stage were massive in size compared to the screen and stage in Tipperary. The movie film was preceded by a show with dancing girls with long legs dressed in frilly clothing! The thought went through my mind wondering what would happen if I let the Tipperary goat loose on that stage! This was during my first week in America before going on to Savannah.

The following week in Savannah, a few of us newly ordained Irish priests went to a cinema dressed as priests. We did not have any other clothes to wear as we arrived from Ireland with only the clothes on our backs. I do not recall the name of that movie film because we were asked to leave the cinema shortly after the movie started. What did we do to deserve this? At that time in Ireland, smoking was allowed in cinemas. We were not aware that it was not allowed in American cinemas. So we lit up our cigarettes and sent rings of smoke into the air. A member of the cinema staff came and ordered us out. He did not give us a chance to explain that we were unaware of the smoking restriction. The cinema was dark, so the audience probably did not notice a group of priests being expelled from the cinema. When we got outside, we stood there on the side of the street like bad boys amused by our surprise expulsion from the cinema. It was certainly something to write home about! I thought of the time many years earlier when I was expelled from the cinema in Tipperary for bringing in a goat!

Shortly after that we were in New Orleans for a six-month orientation program. There we found a solution to the smoking prohibition in cinemas. It was the drive-in movie theatre. This really fascinated us. They seem to have everything in America. Movie drive-in theatres were very plentiful at that time in America. One could drive their car into a large parking area after paying an admission fee at the entrance. There were a few hundred cars parked in rows of parking slots. Cars were parked next to a post, which had a small speaker, which could be mounted inside a car window. Ahead was a massive large screen on which the film was shown. One could watch the film from the comfort of their car. As would be expected, drive-in movie theatres were very popular with courting couples! But for us newly arrived Irish priests, who enjoyed a cigarette, the drive-in theatre was the place to go to watch a film. Drive-in theatres were very common for many years in America, but with the passing of time, they have vanished.

76

ST. MARY ON THE HILL CHURCH

AUGUSTA, GEORGIA

UPON MY RETURN FROM NEW ORLEANS TO THE DIOCESE OF Savannah, I was assigned as an assistant priest—what we call a curate in Ireland—to St. Mary on the Hill Church in Augusta, Georgia. I was one of three priests in the parish. At that time, it had the largest number of parishioners than any parish in the diocese. It had the reputation of being the wealthiest parish in the diocese, and the parishioners were generally very affluent and highly educated. Located within the parish boundary, a short distance from the church, was the world-famous Augusta National Golf Course where the annual Master's Golf Tournament is played. There was also a significant number of military people in the parish, both active and retired. There was a very large military base on the outskirts of the city called Fort Gordon. At that time, the Vietnam War was raging. I officiated at many funerals for young soldiers, who were killed in Vietnam. I found myself frequently doing the best I could to console grieving widows and young children, who had lost a husband and father in war.

During my time at St. Mary's I indicated to the Bishop, my interest in serving for a few years as a missionary in South America with the St. James Society. Some months later, the Pastor (parish priest) at the African-American parish in Augusta asked the Bishop if he could send him an assistant (curate). African-American parishes in the diocese were staffed by priests of The Society of African Missions (SMA). The Bishop contacted me and asked me if I would be willing to go there since it was considered as being mission territory.

I agreed to accept this assignment and became one of the first diocesan priests to be assigned to a parish, which was staffed by priests of the Society of African Missions. When word of my transfer circulated among the parishioners of St. Mary on the Hill parish, some of them were not happy with the news. This was during the period of the Civil Rights movement in the southern states of America. There was much bigotry by white people toward black people. Because of this attitude, some parishioners did not understand why I would accept a transfer from an affluent suburban parish in exchange for an assignment in a parish located in an impoverished area of the city where all the parishioners were black. In spite of this, there were many parishioners who wished me well and assured me of their prayers and support.

77

IMMACULATE CONCEPTION CHURCH

AN AFRICAN-AMERICAN PARISH

AUGUSTA, GEORGIA

I TOOK UP DUTY AT IMMACULATE CONCEPTION AFRICAN-American parish in Augusta in early September 1968. The Pastor (parish priest) was a priest of the Society of African Missions, and I was a diocesan priest. He was subject to his Provincial as well as to the Bishop of Savannah. I was subject to the Bishop of Savannah only. The priest was Father John Sheehan, who was a native of Connecticut. He had spent several years working as a missionary priest in Liberia, West Africa.

I spent three years in that parish until it was merged in June 1971 with two other parishes in Augusta. The other two parishes were Sacred Heart and St. Patrick's, which were "white" middle-class parishes. St. Patrick's Church was chosen as the location for the newly merged parish and was renamed Most Holy Trinity Church to signify the merger of three parishes into one. I spent four more years in that merged parish as an assistant (curate) until my transfer as Pastor (parish priest) to Holy Family Church in Columbus, Georgia.

RIOTS AND DESTRUCTION

ON MONDAY, MAY 11, 1970, WHILE I WAS AT THE AFRICAN American parish in Augusta, riots erupted. A young African American named Charles Oatman, who was a prisoner in the County Jail, was brutally beaten to death. Rumor had it, that the culprits were white prison officers. Because of this, the African American community started rioting, which lasted for two days. Buildings owned by white people were burned along with cars on the streets. Buildings owned by African-Americans were spray-painted to identify them, so they were spared. White people going home from work at the nearby Medical College were attacked and beaten. Several buildings in the area of the Church and School were on fire. The church, school, and convent were spared because of our ministry in the community. Following an investigation into the beating and killing at the jail, two African-American prisoners and other prisoners were convicted.

A ROBUST WOMAN'S WIG

DURING THE TIME WHILE I WAS ASSIGNED TO THE AFRICAN-American parish in Augusta, I formed a Boy Scout troop. Troop 508. I was never a member of the boy scouts. I knew absolutely nothing about the organization. From observing the activities of the scouts in my previous parish, I was anxious to form a group in the African-American parish. I enlisted the help of the scoutmaster from the previous parish. A woman from that parish, who was involved with the scouts as a den mother, also offered to help. This woman was very robust.

At this time, I drove a 1961 Bel-Air station wagon. Typical of American cars during that period, my station wagon was very large and could easily seat about ten passengers. It did not have the luxury of air conditioning or power steering. I solved the air conditioner drawback by having the windshield removed but modified to install it when it rained. With the windshield removed and the rear window open, this created a powerful breeze. It was much better than a convertible car, because by having a roof, the wind coming through had a wind tunnel effect. The faster I drove, the greater was the breeze. I used my station wagon to transport the scouts on various outings. I took them to every Apollo launch at the Kennedy Space Center at Cape Canaveral, Florida. We had the good fortune to witness the blast off of Apollo 11 on July 16, 1969, which resulted in the first lunar landing when Neil Armstrong walked on the moon. On our trips to Cape Kennedy, we camped at a place called Fox Lake Park where we spent the night prior to a launch. When the rocket blasted off, the ground vibrated and sent a tremor through our bodies. Such was the force that sent the rocket into orbit.

On one particular Sunday, the precision flying team of the United States Air Force known as "The Thunderbirds," were putting on an air show at Aiken, South Carolina, which is about a forty-five minute drive from Augusta. I took the scouts to this event. To show my appreciation to the robust woman for all her help, I invited her to come with us. She was delighted to get this opportunity to witness the air display by the famous Thunderbirds. It was a very hot summer day. With the windshield removed and the rear window open, a lovely cool breeze was blowing with a tunnel effect through the station wagon. We enjoyed the air show, but trouble was ahead for me on the return journey.

When leaving Aiken the traffic was backed up, and I was in a hurry to get going as I had to be back in the parish for a youth meeting. As soon as I got away from the traffic, and because I was delayed, I stepped on the accelerator and drove at top speed. The road was a narrow two-lane road, but it had several straight stretches. Then all of a sudden, I heard a siren and saw the blue flashing light of a police car behind me. I stopped for the officer who reprimanded me for speeding. At this period of time in the American south, there were still strong racial tensions between black and white people. When the police officer, who was white was about to issue a speeding ticket, I challenged him by playing the race card. I accused the officer of stopping me for the simple reason that he saw all those black faces in my station wagon. He became very agitated and defensive. I told him that I would report him for being a racist or bigot. He became very nervous and friendly and tried to assure me that he had nothing against black people. When I said that I did not believe him, he told me to be on my way and drive carefully.

This traffic stop delayed me by about ten minutes. I was now very much behind time in my effort to get back to the parish in time for my meeting. When I got going, I was driving very fast. The robust woman, who was in the front seat, pleaded with me to slow down. She was actually crying with fear. Having no windshield and the rear window open, the breeze coming through was like a hurricane. Then all of a sudden, the force of the breeze blew the hair off the head of the robust woman. Dear me, I got a fright because I had no idea that she wore a wig! Her wig blew back into the rear of the station wagon into the hands of the scouts. Needless to say, the scouts thought this was very funny. Having got over the initial shock of finding out that the robust woman wore a wig, I became highly amused at the sight. The wig was now in the hands of the scouts. They were passing it around and trying it on. Then one of the scouts behind me placed the wig on my head!

O Dear Lord! The robust woman was furious and crying and told me that she would report me to the Bishop and do all she could to have my driving license suspended. She retrieved her wig from my head and stuffed it into her purse. I told her she looked much better and younger without the wig. She replied that I would pay dearly for embarrassing her, and she would get her friends to sign a petition requesting the Bishop to have me transferred out of the city of Augusta and as far away as possible. And better still, have me deported back to Ireland! Not a word was spoken during the remainder of the journey. We arrived home, and I was late for the meeting. From then on, the robust woman had nothing to do with me or the scouts.

A few years later I was transferred to Columbus, some two hundred and fifty miles away from Augusta. After a few years in Columbus, I got a surprise phone call from a member of the robust woman's family. They wanted me to know that she had asked to inform me that she was seriously ill and in the hospital and would be very happy if I could come and visit her. I did not hesitate to do this. When I arrived at her bedside, she cried and kissed my hand and told me how much she missed me and all the adventures she had with me. She apologized over the wig incident and began to laugh at how silly it all was. Then with a big smile on her face, she pulled off a wig from her head and threw it up in the air! We both hugged and laughed about the silly incident of some years ago and talked about my station wagon and the scouting adventures. As I was about to leave, she asked me if I would do her a favor? I was humbled when she asked me if I would officiate at her funeral. Some months later, I honored her request.

THE POLICEMAN AND THE CRUCIFIX

IN 1971, WHILE I WAS ASSIGNED TO THE AFRICAN-AMERICAN
parish of Immaculate Conception in Augusta, it was merged
along with the white parish of Sacred Heart into the parish of
St. Patrick. The parish of St. Patrick was then renamed Most
Holy Trinity to signify the three parishes now forming one
parish. Immaculate Conception Church was closed. The
pastor of that church was Father Jack Sheehan. He was transferred to a parish in Savannah. In the sanctuary of Immaculate
Conception Church, there was a very large crucifix with a life-
size body of the crucified Christ mounted on the wall behind
the altar. This crucifix was the personal property of Father
Sheehan. He wanted to take it with him to his new parish in
Savannah. The crucifix was taken down, and the life-size
corpus was removed from the cross. The outstretched arms of
the corpus, which were inserted into the corpus, were also
removed.

Father Sheehan borrowed my Bel Air station wagon to
transport the figure of Jesus to Savannah. The cross and other

personal items of Father Sheehan were transported in a separate vehicle.

The corpus, or figure of Jesus, was placed feet first into my station wagon. The two outstretched arms, which had been removed from the corpus, were placed together by the side of the corpus. A sheet was placed over the corpus. On his way to Savannah with the corpus, he passed through the little town of Waynesboro. On the outskirts of the town, a police car with blue flashing lights and siren blaring, drove up behind him. Father Sheehan pulled in to the side of the road and stopped. The policeman approached the station wagon and told Father Sheen that he was exceeding the speed limit.

While informing Father Sheehan of the reason for the traffic stop, the policeman noticed a "body" with a bloodstained head exposed. During the journey, the sheet had moved leaving the corpus exposed. Thinking it was a corpse, he asked Father Sheehan to explain why he was transporting a corpse. Father Sheehan tried to explain that it was a hand-carved figure of the crucified Christ. The policeman, who was probably of the Baptist religion, would not be familiar with a crucifix. Baptists do not have a figure of Jesus on their crosses. The policeman did not believe Father Sheehan. He ordered him to get out of the station wagon and arrested him. He placed handcuffs on him and put him in the back seat of the police car. He then radioed for backup reporting the discovery of a corpse being transported in a station wagon. Within minutes, several police cars with flashing lights surrounded the station wagon. When the policeman went to the rear of the station wagon to open the door, he noticed the badly bloodstained head of the corpse and exclaimed loudly, "Jesus, this fellow got a terrible death. Look at all the blood on his head." Then when he noticed the two arms side by side on one side of the corpse, he exclaimed, "The misfortunate victim was also dismembered, they cut off his hands." When he touched the corpse, he found it cold and it did not feel like flesh. Upon further examination, the police were satisfied that what appeared to be a corpse was in fact a wooden statue. Father Sheehan was then released from the back seat of the police car, and his handcuffs were removed. The police apologized, and everyone saw the funny side of it. With all the commotion and excitement, Father Sheehan was sent on his way without being issued a speeding ticket!

81

NUNS ARRESTED

DURING MY YEARS AT IMMACULATE CONCEPTION CHURCH and School in Augusta, Georgia, Franciscan nuns staffed the school. Some of them were natives of Ireland. Their convent was located two blocks away from the church and school. One night, when it was a few hours after midnight with everyone in the neighborhood sound asleep, the fire alarm in the school, which was connected to the local fire department, was activated. Fire engines and police cars surrounded the church and school with sirens blaring and lights flashing. I was in a deep sleep and did not hear a sound. The police and firemen tried to alert me, but I was totally unresponsive. They were worried about me and wanted to rescue me from what might be a burning building. When they could not alert me, they decided to go to the convent and have one of the nuns come with a key to enter the house. A police officer drove his car to the convent with siren blaring and blue lights flashing. When the Reverend Mother and another nun responded, the policeman placed the two of them in the back seat of the police car and took off toward the church and school. Because of the sound of the sirens and the flashing lights, the entire neighborhood was now awake. Of course, they noticed the two nuns being placed in the back seat of the police car. When the police and the two nuns arrived at my house, they unlocked the door and went to my bedroom.

When they woke me up from a very deep sleep, I sat up in the bed and saw that I was surrounded by police officers and firemen and the two nuns. One of the firemen shouted at me to get out of bed because the place was on fire. A short time later, it was discovered that there was no fire. The fire alarm system was activated because of some malfunction. By the next morning, word had spread about the two nuns being arrested and placed in the back seat of a police car and taken away. Nobody in the area where the convent was located had known about the false fire alarm further down the street. There was much speculation by the neighbors as to why the two nuns were placed in the back seat of a police car and taken away. Some wondered if the nuns had a fight among themselves during the night. A Protestant neighbor even wondered if the convent was raided by the police because of the possibility that the good nuns might have been operating a house of prostitution! The speculation ended the next morning. The neighbors found out about the fire alarm being activated at the church and school down the street and the police seeking the help of the nuns to rescue a sleeping priest from what they thought may have been a burning building.

82

THE MERGED PARISH OF MOST HOLY TRINITY

AUGUSTA, GEORGIA

IN JUNE OF 1971, FOLLOWING MUCH DISCUSSION, THREE parishes in the downtown area of Augusta were merged into one parish. This was because of a shift in population from the downtown area and the opening of new parishes in the suburbs of the city. The three parishes were Sacred Heart, which was predominantly white with about four hundred families, St. Patrick's, which was predominantly white with about one hundred families, and Immaculate Conception, which was entirely African American with about four hundred families. There were two priests at Sacred Heart, one priest at St. Patrick's, and two priests at Immaculate Conception. Because St. Patrick's Church was in the center of the three parishes and was the oldest parish in the city, it was chosen as the location for the three merged parishes. It would have a combined total parish population of about nine hundred families served by three priests. The church and parish were renamed Most Holy Trinity to signify the merger of the three parishes into one.

There was much understandable anger among the parishioners of the two churches, which were closed. There was also the issue of race. The white people were not ready for integration, and the black people did not want to give up their identity as an African-American congregation, who treasured their own form of worship and song. A priest was brought in from outside of Augusta to be the pastor of the merged parish because he would not be inclined to favor any of the congregations. The assistant priest from Sacred Heart Church and Immaculate Conception Church would remain on as the assistant priests of the merged parish. Father John Sheehan SMA, who was the Pastor of Immaculate Conception Church, was transferred to a parish in Savannah. This was a very challenging undertaking trying to unite the black and white parishioners.

More difficult than uniting the races, was contending with the understandable anger of the parishioners of the closed and very beautiful Sacred Heart Church. The property was eventually sold, and the church building became a cultural center. Immaculate Conception Church building and the Rectory (Presbytery) were converted into a convent for the Franciscan sisters, who staffed Immaculate Conception School. The former convent of the sisters was sold to the city, and it became a rehabilitation center for drug addicts. I remained in this assignment for four years until I was transferred to Holy Family Church in Columbus as pastor in 1975.

83

HOLY FAMILY CHURCH

COLUMBUS, GEORGIA

IN EARLY JUNE OF 1975, I ARRIVED AT HOLY FAMILY CHURCH in Columbus, Georgia, as the new pastor (parish priest). Columbus is two hundred and fifty miles from Augusta. I had a border collie dog and a parakeet bird in a cage. I had looked after this bird for a parishioner in Augusta while she was in the hospital and ended up inheriting it!

While assigned to Holy Family Church in Columbus, I became an American citizen. The date was September 7, 1977. I was ten years in the United States at that time. I was eligible for citizenship after five years of permanent residence. It was not until America celebrated its bicentennial in 1976 that I got the urge to become an American citizen. This allowed me to vote in America and to freely leave and return without any immigration restrictions.

AlSo in the year 1977, I oversaw the restoration of Holy Family Church. This project gave me the experience which helped me to oversee the major restoration of the Cathedral in Savannah twenty-two years later in 1999-2000

My parents died during my years at Holy Family Church in Columbus. My father died suddenly on September 8, 1981. This was only one week after I returned from my annual holidays in Ireland. He was 77 years of age. My mother died on March 17, 1986. She was 71 years of age. May they rest in Peace.

In 1988 I was transferred as Pastor to Blessed Sacrament parish in Savannah. I remained there for eight years until I was transferred as Rector of the Cathedral in Savannah in 1996.

84

MY "HOLLYWOOD" EXPERIENCE

DURING MY YEARS AT HOLY FAMILY CHURCH IN COLUMBUS, I was involved in the making of two movie films. They were *A Time for Miracles* and *A Time to Triumph*.

A Time for Miracles is based on the life of Elizabeth Ann Seton. She was born in New York City in 1774. As a young widow and the mother of five children, she converted to Catholicism. She did this in spite of opposition from her family and friends during a time when Catholics in America were despised. Later on, with the approval of Bishop John Carroll of Baltimore, Maryland, she founded a religious order known as The Sisters of Charity and the first American parochial school. She died in in 1820 at the young age of 46. She was canonized as the first native-born American saint in 1975.

In 1980 film crews from the American Broadcasting Television Network (ABC) arrived in Georgia to make a film based on the life of Elizabeth Ann Seton. She is known as "Mother Seton." The title of the film is *A Time for Miracles*. Filming of the movie took place in Savannah, Columbus, and Westville.

Westville is located thirty miles from Columbus. It is a recon-structed village of the 1850 era. It was a very suitable location for the film because it did not have paved streets, or electric or telephone poles. There was a small timber-framed church in the village as well as an 1850 era timber-framed school.

When the ABC film crew arrived in Columbus, they contacted me at Holy Family Church. They wanted to borrow some church furnishings such as statues, candlesticks, votive candle stands, and a tabernacle. In return, they would make a generous donation to the church. I was delighted to let them borrow all the items on their list, including the statues and a tabernacle. I had a portable tabernacle, which was used each year on Holy Thursday. They had one other request. Because two of the actors were playing the roles of a bishop and a priest, they needed a priest for the position of consultant or technical director. This would entail directing the actor bishop and priest on how to put on vestments and how to conduct Catholic cere-monies. The ceremonies were receiving a convert into the Catholic Church and celebrating Mass and giving Holy Communion to a First Communion group. The Mass had to be according to the Latin Mass ritual of pre-Vatican II. The vest-ments were in the Roman style in use during that period. Now that they were in my church and getting a loan of church furnishing from me, I was an obvious choice for this position. When offered this position, I did not hesitate to accept. After all, this was my chance to have a "Hollywood" experience! I would then be employed by the film crew, and there was going to be a generous stipend offered for my time and consultation! I could not believe my luck! It was also going to be an opportu-nity to mingle with famous actors.

Being a technical advisor or consultant for the film crew

involved a few hours each day from me for a about a week. On the first day of my movie film career, I drove the thirty miles to the 1850 era reconstructed village of Westville. I was introduced to the cast. The role of Mother Seton was played by Kate Mulgrew, who was well known for her television role as Mrs. Columbo. The role of Bishop John Carroll of Baltimore was played by Lorne Green of *Bonanza* fame. The role of the priest was played by Milo O'Shea, who was a well- known actor and radio and television personality in Ireland. I felt very privileged to be working side by side with such famous actors. I have treasured pictures of myself taken with those actors.

Being a person, who likes mischief and excitement, loaning the church furnishings to the film crew gave me an opportunity to play a prank on my parishioners. When they came to church for weekday and weekend Masses, they were shocked and stunned to find that the statues and votive candle stands were missing. Since I had not told anyone abut loaning these items to the film crew, I pretended that they were stolen! This caused great alarm and consternation in the parish. When asked if this was reported to the police, I assured them that an investigation was under way. I had already tipped off the Police Chief about my prank just in case others notified the police. The Police Chief went along with my prank. Parishioners were very upset and all this became the talk of the city. When the media got involved, I decided that I had enough fun. But I did not want to let it be known that it was a prank. The borrowed items were now ready to be returned. I arranged to have them returned late at night when parishioners and neighbors were in their homes and would not see the delivery. They were brought into the church by the side door in the parking lot. When word got out that the items were returned, I did not want to come clean and tell what happened. Instead, I pretended that the "thieves" got nervous thinking that God would punish them for stealing church property, and they returned everything on condition that I would not reveal their identity or press any changes against them. The parishioners were happy that the items were returned safely.

My second "Hollywood" experience was in Columbus in 1985, when I appeared briefly in a scene baptizing a baby. The title of the move was *A Time to Triumph*. The film tells the true story of Concetta and Charles Hassan. They had three children. She joined the army to support their family after her husband was disabled. She became a helicopter pilot. The location for the film was at Columbus and the nearby Army Infantry Base at Fort Benning. The role of Concetta Hassan was played by Patty Duke. The role of her husband, Charles Hassan, was played by Joe Bologna.

After arrival in Columbus to make the movie, the film crew came to Holy Family Church to meet with me and ask a favor. They wanted to use the church for a baptism scene for one of the children of Charles and Concetta Hassan. I was more than happy to oblige. So instead of finding someone to play the role of the priest performing the baptism, it occurred to them that since they were speaking with a real priest and using his church for the baptism, they may as well get the real priest to play the role. I was delighted to be offered this role. So once again, Hollywood, here I come! This was going to be exciting because I was going to be co-starring with Patty Duke—even though the scene was going to be very brief.

Later on, the filming crew decided that the location of the baptism font at Holy Family Church was not in a suitable location for their cameras. They looked elsewhere. They found the location of the baptism font at nearby St. Luke United Methodist Church to be ideal. The baptism scene was moved to St. Luke's United Methodist Church, but since the baptism was a Catholic ceremony, I still had the role of the priest in the ceremony. After the baptism scene, a picture appeared in the Columbus Ledger newspaper the next day taken on the steps of St. Luke United Methodist Church. It shows Patty Duke holding the baby, and I am standing next to her. This picture is among my treasured collections. I am waiting for another "Hollywood" experience!

PRAY FOR THE POPE

HOLY FAMILY CHURCH IN COLUMBUS, WHERE I WAS PASTOR
for thirteen years, was surrounded by four other churches. They
were Baptist, Methodist, Presbyterian, and Episcopal. That area
of Columbus was known as "Church Square" because of the
number of churches located next to each other. Holy Family
Church was the only one that had its own parking lot, which
was capable of holding around one hundred cars. The other
churches had to settle for street parking on Sundays. First
Baptist Church had its own parking lot in later years. Adjacent
to Holy Family Church was the Baptist Church. On Sundays,
the Baptists had a tendency to park their cars in Holy Family's
parking lot.

The five churches had a wonderful relationship with each
other. This was due mainly to the fact that members of each
church were married to members of one of the other churches.
We shared many things between each other as well as attending
functions together. The only thing I was not willing to share
was allowing the other churches to share our parking lot on

Sunday mornings. This would cause many of our parishioners to have to find street parking. To identify the cars of Holy Family parishioners, I issued each family a decal to place on the lower passenger side of their car windshield. The decal had the letters HFC that indicated they belonged to Holy Family Church. So when the parking lot was full to capacity on a Sunday, the ushers could easily identify the cars from other churches. Because the Baptist Church was located right next to our parking lot, they were usually the ones who used our parking lot, thinking that they were not noticed.

I was very friendly with the Pastor of the Baptist Church, so I decided to have a chat with him and ask him to beg his members to refrain from using our parking lot on Sundays. I also decided to get his attention and the attention of his members by pretending that I would place bumper stickers on the cars of his members. Knowing how Baptists feel about the Pope, I told him that the bumper sticker would read—PRAY FOR THE POPE. This got his attention, and he assured me that he would make regular announcements from his pulpit warning his people about the consequences of using the Catholic parking lot. Even though I was only bluffing him, he took me seriously and made regular pulpit announcements. His members took the announcements seriously and stopped encroaching on our parking lot—at least for the time being. Gradually, they started to return. Because I did not really want to place bumper stickers on their cars, I had to come up with another idea to keep them out. What did I do? I had large posters printed, which read as follows:

The Pope is grateful for the prayers of First
Baptist Church.

Please continue to pray for the Roman Catholic
Pontiff.

I had the ushers place those posters on the windshield of
every car in our parking lot that did not have the HFC decal.
After a few Sundays, we had no more Baptist cars in our
parking lot. The Baptist minister phoned me to say that he
warned his members not to use our parking lot, and that they
should be glad that all they got was a poster on their windshield
instead of a sticker on their bumper. Then he went on to tell
me that he, along with several members of his congregation,
actually found my tactic very amusing and to convey his best
wishes to the Pope!

86

A LADY METHODIST MINISTER

As seen in previous stories, during my years in Columbus, Georgia, from 1975 to 1988, a wonderful spirit existed between the Catholic Church and the local Protestant churches. Many of our members were intermarried with members of each of the other churches. It was our custom during the summer months to cancel Sunday evening services and hold service in just one church. There were five churches involved. All five churches were next door to each other. The churches were First Baptist, St. Luke United Methodist, First Presbyterian, Trinity Episcopal, and Holy Family Catholic. The pastors of each church participated in the service, which consisted of singing, prayers, scripture readings, and a sermon. One rule was that no pastor could give the sermon in his church. At a planning meeting in advance, pastors were selected for preaching at particular churches. The host pastor planned the service for his church and assigned roles to the pastors who would not be giving the sermon.

One summer, the senior pastor of St. Luke United Methodist Church, Rev. Dr. Donald M. Kea, was assigned to give the sermon at Holy Family Catholic Church. Shortly before the due date for preaching, Dr. Kea informed us that he would not be available due to an unexpected matter he had to attend to. Because it was St. Luke United Methodist's turn to preach at Holy Family Catholic Church, the recently graduated and newly ordained female associate pastor of St Luke's, the Reverend Cindy Cox, would have to take his place.

This could pose a problem for me as pastor of Holy Family Church. The Catholic Church does not ordain women or welcome their preaching. I was very aware that a large segment of my congregation was very set in their ways and would not be in favor of permitting a female minister to give the sermon at our church. But as I saw it, life is full of surprises, and we do what we have to do. There was no way I would allow our good relationship with the other churches to deteriorate by forbidding Reverend Cindy Cox to preach. I figured that maybe God was trying to tell us Roman Catholics something. The Roman Catholic Church was not going to disintegrate by allowing a sincere young female Methodist minister to preach. It would be a new experience for us and would enhance our relationship with the local Protestant churches.

When the time came for Reverend Cindy Cox to preach, I went to the microphone and with my best Irish charm, I informed the Catholics in the congregation that we were going to make history that evening by having a woman deliver the sermon. I explained why she was going to preach instead of the Pastor of St. Luke's Methodist Church. I introduced Rev. Cindy Cox and invited her to come to the pulpit to deliver the sermon. She preached an outstanding sermon. After the service was over, I heard nothing but the highest compliments from Catholics for allowing this young and dynamic lady Methodist minister to preach and give our congregation at Holy Family Roman Catholic Church a new and refreshing experience!

87

MY TWELVE CHILDREN

As mentioned in the previous story, several other Protestant churches surrounded Holy Family Church in Columbus, Georgia, where I spent thirteen years. I was very friendly with the ministers of all the churches. I left Columbus in 1988 for Savannah but made periodic return visits. As the years went by, the ministers at those churches had changed except for the Reverend Cindy Cox Garrard, who was the assistant minister at St. Luke's Methodist Church. This was the Methodist minister mentioned in the previous story, who preached at Holy Family Catholic Church. During one particular visit back to Columbus some thirty years after I had left there for Savannah, I made an unannounced visit to St. Luke's Methodist Church, hoping to meet her.

I arrived at the church office dressed casually. The office receptionist had no idea who I was. I decided to play a little game! On arrival, she greeted me and asked if she could assist me. Looking very serious, I told her that my work had brought me to Columbus and that I would like to become a member of

St. Luke's Methodist Church. She was delighted and assured me that I would be very welcome. When she started to get information from me, such as my name, address, and names of family members, I told her that before doing this I had some questions to ask. I asked her if the church had room in their Sunday School program for the large number of children that I had. She asked me how many children I had. I replied that I had twelve children! She gasped on hearing this and looked astonished. When she regained her composure, she remarked that was a lot of children to feed and clothe. I went on to say that my wife had four sets of triplets and that she was pregnant again and I had no idea how many more might be in the next batch! She kept looking at me, trying to absorb what I was telling her.

I was standing there with a straight face and enjoying her reaction. But in my Irish humor, I decided to add something more. I told her that I had a serious problem, which might prevent me from becoming a member of the Methodist Church. She looked at me with compassion and assured me that the church was there to help people with problems. I went on to say my problem was a very serious one, and that I did not want anyone in the congregation to know about it. She assured me that it would be confidential. I informed her that my wife was a Methodist and that I was a Roman Catholic priest with twelve children and that the Bishop knew nothing about this and that he was appointing me as the pastor of Holy Family Church across the street! The church receptionist got such a shock that I thought she was going to fall off her chair. When she recovered from this, she was very confused. She told me that she did not know how to handle this situation, and that I should talk with the pastor or senior minister. I told her I would love to discuss this with him. She informed me that he was not in that day, but that the Assistant Minister, the Reverend Cindy Cox Garrard, was in her office. I agreed to meet with the Reverend Cindy.

The receptionist got up from her desk looking confused and went to an adjoining room, leaving the door open. I could hear lots of laughter in the room. After a few minutes, the Revered Cindy appeared with a big smile on her face. On seeing me, she said that she knew it had to be me because who else would have such an outrageous story! We had a good laugh about all this, and I apologized to the receptionist for making up such a story. She took it in good spirits and saw the humor in it. After a lovely visit with the Reverend Cindy Cox Garrard, I got into my car and drove the two hundred and fifty miles back to Savannah amused by my silly prank!

88

WOMAN SHOWS HER KNICKERS IN CHURCH

DURING MY TIME AT HOLY FAMILY CHURCH IN COLUMBUS, there was a woman who was rather large in size. She was very domineering and aggressive. She was also a reader at Mass. One Sunday before Mass, she stopped by my office to discuss something with me. On her way to Mass through the house, which was attached to the church, she made a visit to the toilet. When it was time for the reading at Mass she came out from her pew and walked up to the pulpit. Her skirt was tucked inside her knickers, and her very large rear end was exposed! Sitting in my chair, I could see the amusement and shock on the faces of the people sitting in the pews. How was I going to handle this? I had to do something to prevent her from going back to the pew after the reading and coming up again for Holy Communion with her underwear exposed. While she was reading, I walked over and stood next to the pulpit. At the end of the reading, I tried to whisper to her that she should pull her skirt out from inside her knickers. But by the time I got her attention, she was right out in front of the altar making a solemn bow with her exposed backside toward the congregation. Oh, what a sight! Finally, when I got her attention, she calmly removed her skirt from inside her knickers. Then she turned around to the congregation, took another bow, and made her way back to her pew. She was a good sport! I had to keep my composure during my sermon which followed!

89

GROOM VANISHES DURING HIS
WEDDING

EVERY WEDDING IS DIFFERENT AND ANYTHING CAN HAPPEN. I was officiating at a wedding in Columbus when the groom got up and walked out during my homily. I did not take much notice of this. He might not have been feeling well or maybe wanted to use the toilet. I was in the pulpit talking away about how happy we were for the couple on their special day. But the groom was gone so long that I got worried, and I was repeating myself, wishing that he would return. I motioned to his best man to go into the sacristy and check on him. He might have fainted and passed out with nerves. The best man then was gone so long, and I was sounding foolish repeating myself in an effort to play for time until the groom and best man returned. My worst fears were realized when the best man stood at the sacristy door and indicated that the groom was missing. I got down from the pulpit and spoke with the best man, who confirmed that the groom could not be found. Dear me!! This wedding was certainly going to be different!

I approached the bride and as tactfully and gently as I

could, and I informed her that the groom had vanished. She looked at me in disbelief and asked me if I was joking. When I told her that it was not a joke, but was for real, she burst out crying. All her makeup was running down her face with the tears and on to her lovely bridal dress. Then all the bridesmaids started crying and wailing. Then they all got around the bride trying to console her. I had to announce to the congregation that the groom had run away. There were gasps throughout the church. Then the bride's mother stood up and turned towards the groom's father and mother on the other side of the aisle. She screamed in a loud voice looking directly at them saying, "I knew he was no good." The groom's father did not take kindly to this accusation, so he shouted back at the bride's mother saying, "Your daughter is a spoiled *****." Then both families came out of their pews in to the aisle, verbally attacking each other. There was absolute pandemonium in the church with insults and tempers out of control. In the meantime, the bride got weak and had to get medical help from a doctor who was in the church, thankfully as a guest of the bride's family. After everyone left the church, the floor was littered with bridal flowers as well as some items of bridal clothing. The fighting continued outside on the steps of the church and, of course, attracted an audience of onlookers. I heard later that there was no wedding reception, but the cost of the reception was not cancelled. This of course added to the tension between both families.

The groom was from another city and state several hundreds of miles away. After some time, he phoned me to explain why he vanished from his own wedding ceremony. He told me that they broke off a previous relationship when they lived in the same city in another state. They broke up and went their separate ways because the bride had a problem with alcohol. After a few years apart, they got back together when it appeared that she had overcome her addiction and was sober for a few years. They decided to get married. On the day of the wedding, when she walked up the aisle and arrived at the altar, there was a strong smell of alcohol from her. He felt betrayed but took his seat to think things over during the opening part of the ceremony. After the scripture readings, and by the time I got up to give my homily, he had made up his mind to walk away. He considered this was a more practical option than having to go through a divorce later. He had given up on her and lost trust and confidence in her. He left the altar and went into the sacristy and out to the street and got a taxi to his hotel to collect his belongings and then went to the airport and flew home. I never heard from him again. The bride, who lived in the parish, eventually moved away and I never heard from her again.

90

NIGHT CALL BY A POLICEWOMAN

ONE NIGHT WHEN I WAS AT HOLY FAMILY CHURCH IN Columbus, Georgia, several hours after I had gone to bed and was sound asleep, I was awakened by the barking of my dog. I heard the sound of the doorbell and thought to myself that at that hour of night it had to be a beggar or a drunk looking for help. I decided not to go down stairs to check and tried to go back to sleep. But the dog kept barking, and the doorbell kept ringing. I got out of bed to go down the stairs to the front door. The front door had frosted glass and had a light on outside. About halfway down the stairs I could see an outline of a person in the light, and I could hear what seemed like several voices talking. I did not answer the door thinking it was a bunch of drunks, and it would be difficult to get rid of them. I went back to bed again. But the dog kept on barking, and the doorbell kept ringing.

Overhead the front door was a balcony with an iron railing. I went out on the balcony to find out who was at the door below. I usually sleep with no clothes on, and thinking that the people at the door were a bunch of drunks, I did not see any need to get dressed. I was totally naked! I shouted out to whoever was at the door to come out where I could see them. To my surprise a policewoman stepped out! The voices I had been hearing at the door when I was on the stairs were coming from her radio. She looked up at me, startled at the sight of my naked body, and I looked down at her apologizing for not being dressed. She told me that she called to let me know that she saw some homeless people going into the church, and on checking it, she found it was not locked. She was concerned because the homeless people were smoking cigarettes inside the church. I asked her to wait, and that I would get dressed and come down to her. The house was attached to the church. I apologized for being undressed and assured her that I was not trying to put on an exhibition for her at that hour of the night. Actually, she seemed quite amused by this! We went into the church together and checked it out and locked the doors. I thanked her for her concern and for being so diligent in looking out for any suspicious activity. I bid her good night and went back to bed, very amused by my naked encounter with the policewoman!

Several weeks later I went to a local restaurant on a Saturday evening for my dinner. There was a group of people sitting at a table nearby. I did not take any notice of them. When they got up to leave, one of them, a lady, came over to me and asked me if I remembered her? I had absolutely no idea who she was. To my surprise, she informed me that she was the policewoman, who got me out of bed some time ago. I did not recognize her because she looked very different without a police uniform and cap and she had her hair let down. When she told me who she was, I replied that I was glad she recognized me with my clothes on!

91

A LOAN FROM THE BISHOP

BECAUSE OF A SERIOUS HEARING LOSS IN BOTH EARS, I HAD TO get hearing aids. The cost was fifteen hundred dollars. Hearing aids were not covered by my health insurance. I could not afford this. Considering my hearing loss to be a professional hazard, I decided to phone my Bishop and ask him for a loan of fifteen hundred dollars. At that time, I was living in Columbus, Georgia, and the Bishop was living in Savannah, Georgia, a distance of two hundred and fifty miles. The Bishop at that time, was of French background and was a very stern man, who did not fully appreciate the Irish sense of humor!

When I got the Bishop on the phone, I told him that I needed a loan of fifteen hundred dollars. He asked why I needed the loan. To make sure that he was aware of my hearing loss, I pretended that I did not hear what he said. So I asked him to repeat what he just said. He replied that he asked me why I needed the loan. I told him that I needed to get hearing aids. Then he asked why did I need the hearing aids? What a silly question to ask! My Irish humor took over, and I replied

223

that it was because my eyesight was bad! He did not appreciate this answer and reprimanded me for trying to be funny. I replied that I thought he was trying to be funny by asking me why I needed hearing aids.

I went on to explain that I had a serious hearing loss and that this was a problem in dealing with people. Again, my Irish humor took over, and I went on to tell him that whenever a woman came to my office to discuss something personal that it was very difficult for me to hear her while sitting behind my desk. I went on to tell him that the only way I could hear her was to get up from behind my desk and go and sit near her and ask her to come close to my ear so that I could hear her. The Bishop got very upset on hearing this and warned me that this could be misunderstood. I responded by saying that was why I needed a loan for hearing aids. Now that he seemed to be getting concerned about my reputation, I decided to go a step further to increase his concern.

I told him that when I fail to hear a woman sitting close to me, I invited her to sit on my knee and talk right into my ear. The Bishop got really upset on hearing this. He was speaking so loudly that I had to hold the phone away from my deaf ear! I asked him to calm down and help me. I went on to add some more Irish humor by saying that the women were generally very overweight, and I tended to suffocate under them and had to get them off my knee! He finally saw this as amusing and indicated that I had to be making this up. Now that I had gotten his attention on the hazards of my loss of hearing, we were able to discuss the possibility of a loan. I pointed out to him the dangers I was facing in dealing with women, who came to my office to discuss their personal matters. I stated that one had to do what had to be done, and that my situation was what it was.

I went on to tell him that it was up to him as to whether or not he should give me the loan or put my reputation at risk.

He agreed to give me an interest-free loan payable in monthly installments. I indicated that it would be difficult for me to make the monthly payments on this large amount. I asked him if he would pay half the cost and loan me the other half, which I could manage to pay off. My Irish humor got the better of me again, so I said to the Bishop that if he paid for one hearing aid, I would use that hearing aid for hearing mortal sins in his honor and the other hearing aid for hearing venial sins in honor of the loan. He was not amused by this suggestion. However, he did take the risk of my professional hazard seriously and agreed to pay half of the cost and let me have a loan on the other half. Having done better than I had expected in securing a loan and having to pay only half of the total cost, I wished him well, and we terminated the phone call while I was ahead.

92

THE WOMAN WHO MARRIED THE SEVEN BROTHERS

In the twenty-second chapter of the Gospel according to Matthew, we read about the woman who married the seven brothers. The Sadducees, who believed that there was no resurrection, asked Jesus whose wife she will be at the resurrection since all seven brothers had married her. On a Sunday when this was the reading from the Gospel, there was a man from the parish at Mass. His wife had died, and he was planning to marry a widow from the parish. On the way out from Mass, he told me that he found the Gospel reading very upsetting. We arranged a date and time for him to come to my office so that we could discuss it.

When we met, he told me that the Gospel reading upset him because his wife had died, and he was planning to get married again to a widow. He would always consider his deceased wife as his only wife. He could not see where the second wife would fit into the picture in the next world. I pointed out to him that he was not paying attention to the answer that Jesus gave to the Sadducees. Jesus said that in the next world there would be no marriage. This did not help him. He got more upset saying he did not agree with Jesus! That in the next world his first wife would still be his wife. He did not know what he would do with the second wife in the next world. This conversation was getting out of hand. We were getting no place. So in desperation, I suggested that if he did not bother getting married to the widow, then he would have no problems in the next world. This upset him more. He said that he really wanted to marry the widow. So I said that since she is going to be such a problem for him in the next world, why get married to her. He replied that she would be useful to him. This answer annoyed me. I accused him of being devious because he was going to use her.

I went on to ask him if he had told the widow that the reason he wanted to marry her was because she would be useful to him. He replied that he had not. I insisted that he had to tell her this. If he did not tell her, I would refuse to officiate at the wedding. I gave him one week to tell her this, and then get back to me, and let me know her response. I told him that if she was still willing to marry him, then she deserved what she was getting! He left my office now more upset than he was when he came in. After a week went by, I did not hear from him, so I phoned him to ask him if he had told the widow that she would be useful to him. He had not done it. I asked him if he still wanted to marry the widow. He did. So I arranged a date and time for the two of them to meet with me.

They both arrived in my office holding hands and looking very romantic. After some small talk, I decided to get to the purpose of the meeting. I asked him if he had told the widow what I asked him to tell her. He replied that he had not. The widow then asked if there was something she needed to know.

When I said there was, the man got very restless and looked at me as if pleading with me not to tell her. I told her that the primary reason why this man wanted to marry her was because she would be useful to him. She looked stunned. She sat silently for a moment. The silence in my office was deafening! As soon as she absorbed what I had told her, she stood up. She walked up behind his chair and gave him a powerful slap across the side of his head. I thought his head would fall off. She asked me for a telephone directory and if she could use the phone on my desk. She phoned a taxi and stomped out of my office without saying a word. The man sat there staring at me with anger on his face. He was angry at me for what I did. I told him that I believed this was best for both of them. Then I could not resist adding that he will not have any problems in the next world because, if they all went to heaven, his first wife would hand him over to the Devil for bringing a second wife with him. He left my office without saying a word and lived for several years after that without a second wife.

About two years later, the widow phoned me to set up an appointment with me. She came to tell me that she had met another man. They were considering marriage. She asked me if I would meet with him and see if I would recommend him as a suitable husband. I met with the man and spent a few hours interrogating him. I phoned the widow to tell her that as far as I could determine, I considered him to be genuine. A date was arranged for the marriage. During one of my meetings with both of them, the widow asked me if I could manage to take about ten days off after the wedding. They were taking a cruise to the Virgin Islands for their honeymoon and would like to take me along with them! I enjoyed the cruise!

93

AN ABUSIVE HUSBAND

During my years in Columbus, a woman in the parish complained to me about her husband. She told me that on Friday nights he drank too much and became abusive. He often beat her. She was afraid to report him to the police. This would only make things worse for her. I asked her permission to talk with her husband about this. She agreed. I contacted the husband, and he agreed to meet with me in my office.

After a long discussion, I came to the conclusion that he was going to continue his Friday night drinking binges. At that time, I was young and in fairly good physical condition. I told him that if he ever beat his wife again, I would beat him myself, and I might get some men in the parish to help me. When he indicated that he did not believe I would do this, I warned him that I was very serious about it. He left my office in the same frame of mind as he arrived.

On a Friday night a few weeks later, one of his children phoned me to tell me that their father was drunk and was beating their mother. I told the child that I would go over to

229

the house. When I arrived, I found a very drunken man who was out of control. I grabbed him by his shirt and hit him a few punches. It was an easy deal with him because he was drunk and unable to keep his balance. I managed to drag him into the bathroom. I threw him into the bathtub and turned on the water while holding his head under the faucet. He was so drunk that there was no way he could defend himself. When the tub filled up, I stuck his head under the water a few times. He was screaming and cursing and swearing. His wife then pleaded with me to stop and not to hurt him. I was so mad at her for interfering that I told her that I would do the same to her and that maybe they deserved each other. I left the man in the tub and told the wife she could take it from there. All the children were crying. As I was leaving the house, I said, "This is the way I do marriage counseling." I left the house thinking I should never get involved between a man and his wife. One minute they can be killing each other and the next minute kissing each other. Let them sort it out themselves. I went home and went to bed, more annoyed with the wife than I was with the abusive husband. I think she deserved him.

The next morning, Saturday, the abusive husband phoned me to request a meeting with him as soon as possible. I agreed to meet him that afternoon. When he arrived in my office, he complained of having a very sore head. He also let me know that the contents in his wallet were soaked with water from his time in the bathtub. I told him to be glad that they were his only problems and how I was tempted to drown him! Only for the fact that I would be charged with attempted murder, and his wife's interference, I would have kept his head under the water for a much longer time. I was expecting him to be very angry with me. Instead, he started to whimper like a little puppy dog being reprimanded. He expressed his apology and told me that he was very ashamed of his conduct. He blamed it all on the drink and promised that he would never again drink to excess. I told him that was not enough because one drink would lead to another, and another. I demanded that he give up the drink completely. Then I issued a warning. I told him that if I ever heard of him drinking again, then I would arrange with some connections that I had to take him out into the woods for a flogging. I was only bluffing, but since he had already experienced my following through on my threat to beat him up if he ever beat his wife again, he took me seriously this time. After we talked for some more time, and with lots of tears from his eyes and promises to change his ways, he left my office asking me to pray for him. He never touched a drink after that.

It is the custom in the Diocese of Savannah for the Bishop to hold a special Mass at the Cathedral in Savannah on the Sunday closest to Valentine's Day for married couples in the diocese who are celebrating Silver and Golden Jubilee of marriage. Several years after I was transferred from Columbus to Savannah, this former abusive husband and his wife were among those at a Mass celebrating their Silver Jubilee of marriage! They were still happily married, and he has never touched a drink since that night when I was tempted to drown him in the bathtub.

94

BLESSED SACRAMENT CHURCH

SAVANNAH, GEORGIA

I ARRIVED AT BLESSED SACRAMENT CHURCH IN SAVANNAH from Holy Family Church in Columbus on August 25, 1988. That was exactly twenty-one years to the day since I first arrived in America. It took me a long time to settle in Savannah, which was two hundred and fifty miles from Columbus. I did not know anyone, and I was totally unknown. Blessed Sacrament Church and School are located in a very affluent area of the city. The street next to the church, Victory Drive, is one of the most beautiful in the city. The median is lined with palm trees and covered with azalea blossoms in springtime. Across the street from the church is 80-acre Daffin Park, where I took my two border collies for walks. I had one assistant priest (curate) and two other priests living with me.

It took me several months to get to know the parishioners. Because there were six exits from the church, and because people tended to use the same exit and entrance, I tried to rotate which door to stand at in an effort to meet as many parishioners as possible. I begged them to get to know me.

After being there for three months, I went back to Columbus one weekend to officiate at a wedding. On the following Sunday at each Mass, I asked the congregation from the pulpit if they missed me the previous weekend. I decided to make up a story to get their attention. I told them that when I went back to Columbus there were traffic jams in the city because of people trying to meet me. They were kissing and hugging me so much and telling me how much they missed me! Then I added that when the time would come for my transfer, they will miss me just like the people in Columbus! After that I think I had won them over! I celebrated my Silver Jubilee of ordination in 1992 while I was at Blessed Sacrament. When some people came from Columbus to my jubilee, Blessed Sacrament parishioners kept telling them that Savannah was now my home!

There was a large elementary school (primary) at Blessed Sacrament. In previous years, it was staffed by the Sisters of Mercy. But due to declining vocations to religious life there were no sisters teaching when I was there. All the teachers were lay people. The school principal operated a very good school with high expectations from the students. She usually took care of discipline. However, whenever there was a serious breach in discipline by a student, she called on me. I am not sure if she realized that I was not much help in that regard. While trying to take care of the situation, I was often amused but had to pretend that I was not amused! An example of this was when one day a student hoisted a bicycle up to the top of the flag pole. The Principal summoned me to come out and reprimand the students. I had to pretend that I was annoyed when in fact I was amused by it. It was like something I would have done myself when I was a student. There were several other occasions when I had to look annoyed when I was actually amused.

But there were a few occasions when I was actually annoyed. One of the times was when a student flushed a girl's bra down the toilet during a basketball game in the school gymnasium. It blocked up the pumping system to the sewer. The locker rooms and toilets were below ground. The contents in the septic tank had to be pumped up into the sewer system. Because the pump was clogged up, and the contents of the full septic tank were flowing out and the level was rising, it was going to damage the air conditioner chiller. I had to call the plumber. He was up to his ankles in smelly human waste. After removing a section of the pump, he found that a cloth was tightly wrapped around the mechanism. Using plyers, he took the cloth apart piece by piece. It turned out to be a girl's bra. He said the student, who did this, should be expelled from the school.

I was determined to find the culprit. This probably happened during the basketball game. The next day I rounded up all the students in the gymnasium and told them I had hidden cameras installed and that I knew who flushed the bra down the toilet. I told them that if the student who did it would admit it, he or she would not be punished for telling the truth. But if nobody admits it, then the person I saw on camera doing it will be expelled. My bluff worked! One student admitted doing it and apologized. The student was the PLUMBER'S son!

At the end of August 1996, after eight years at Blessed Sacrament Church and School, I was transferred to the Cathedral of St. John the Baptist in Savannah as rector where I would spend the next seventeen years until retirement in 2013.

95

MY UNCLE IN BROOKLYN

MY UNCLE, DANNY O'NEILL, LIVED IN BROOKLYN, NEW York. When I arrived home one Saturday afternoon while I was at Blessed Sacrament Church in Savannah, my assistant priest (curate) was in the church hearing confessions. He left a note under the door of my office, which read:

YOUR UNCLE IN BROOKLYN IS DEAD. DON'T BOTHER CALLING

This came as a great shock to me. I was puzzled as to why I was not to bother calling the family. In any case, I phoned his daughter Sheila with whom he lived. There was no answer. I thought she might be at the hospital. Then I called another one of his daughters, Kathleen, who lived out on Long Island. When she answered the phone, I offered her my sympathies on the death of her father. She got a terrible shock and did not know what I was talking about. Then she got upset that nobody from the family had phoned her about her father's unexpected death. I told her about the written message that my assistant had left for me. She then phoned his house in Brooklyn and got no answer. In panic, she drove all the way from Long Island into Brooklyn to find out what happened to her father. When she arrived at the house in tears, she found her sister Sheila in the kitchen. When she asked what happened to her father and how he died, Shelia did not understand this. She assured Kathleen that her father was alive and well. Kathleen then explained about the phone call she got from me and the news of her father's death. Sheila was confused as to how I would have known that he died since I was living nearly a thousand miles away. Sheila then goes upstairs to check on her father and could not find him. Concern arose that maybe her father was found dead on the street and might have had a note on him to phone me in case of an emergency. She phoned me to clarify how I found out about the death. I explained about the note that my assistant wrote for me. Panic now set in because her father was missing and reported as being dead. All other members of the family were notified about this. Within a short time, every member of the family had arrived at the house from wherever they lived. Where was their father? Local hospitals and police were contacted but no information was available.

It being a Saturday evening, it occurred to them that maybe their father had walked to evening mass at nearby Our Lady of Angels Church. They went up to the church and went straight to the pew where my uncle usually sat. There he was engrossed in prayer with his Rosary Beads. He was surprised by the sudden and unexpected arrival of so many family members. They ordered him to come outside with them. When they got outside, they told him that they got word that he was dead. He could not understand how they got this information. They explained to him about my phone call from Savannah telling them that he was dead. My uncle was very amused by all of this, but the family was in no mood for amusement. They wanted to get to the bottom of this story. Upon further questioning they found out from him that he had tried to phone me earlier in the day. He explained that he left a message with someone at my place. When asked what his message was, he stated as follows:

"TELL WILLIE OLIVER THAT HIS UNCLE IN BROOKLYN IS GOING TO BED. DON'T BOTHER CALLING BACK."

Now the story began to make some sense. My assistant (curate) was a native of Iowa, and my uncle Danny, even after almost fifty years in America, still spoke with a very thick Irish brogue. So my assistant misunderstood the word "bed" for "dead."

When my uncle Danny arrived back at his house from the church, he was highly amused to find so many people had already gathered to mourn his passing! The family then phoned me to let me know about the misunderstanding. Later I asked my assistant to tell me what exactly the phone message was. He told me that someone with a very strong accent phoned asking for me. When he told this person that I was not home, he was told to tell me that my uncle in New York is dead and not to bother calling back. Some years later, I was notified that my uncle was in hospital, and death was imminent. When I did get the call that he had died, I wanted to be sure that he was really dead this time! May he rest in Peace.

96

CATHEDRAL OF ST. JOHN THE BAPTIST

SAVANNAH, GEORGIA

I TOOK UP DUTY AS RECTOR OF THE CATHEDRAL OF ST. JOHN the Baptist in Savannah on August 28, 1996. This was a ten-minute drive from my previous residence at Blessed Sacrament Church. This assignment was the most interesting of all my assignments. The Cathedral is a very large building with twin spires. It seats one thousand people and is usually full at all three Sunday Masses and the Saturday evening Vigil Mass. Because Savannah is a popular tourist destination, many of the people at Mass are visitors, who come from various parts of the world. There are two daily weekday Masses at the Cathedral.

During the years 1999-2000, the Cathedral underwent a major restoration. The cost of this project was almost twelve million dollars. I really enjoyed the challenge of overseeing this project. Each day, I climbed the scaffolding to inspect the work. Elsewhere in this book, I will include stories relating to this restoration project.

I remained as Rector of the Cathedral until June 2013 when

I retired. Retirement was not easy for me, but I had to do this because of health reasons, especially a heart attack in 2011. I continue to live in retirement at the Cathedral and plan to do so until the end of my time on this earth.

97

MY PANTS FELL OFF

I WAS TOTALLY INVOLVED IN THE CATHEDRAL RESTORATION project. Each day I was on site, climbing scaffolding to check on the work. I wanted to see for myself instead of getting a report from someone else. The Cathedral has twin spires, each being 207 feet in height. The cross on top of each spire gives an additional seven feet in height. Scaffolding surrounded the exterior of the Cathedral. The twin spires had thirty-one decks of scaffolding all the way to the very top. There was a built-in stairwell in the scaffolding as far as the roofline. The scaffolding around the spires had a ladder attached. When climbing the spires, one had to wear a safety harness. I climbed the spires many times.

On the morning of January 2, 2000, while at the desk in my office, the project foreman came to inform me about a serious structural problem near the top of one of the spires. Because I had to examine this myself, I dashed out and climbed up the built-in stairwell going to the roofline. I then got on the ladder to climb up the exterior of the spires. In my haste, I forgot to put on my safety harness. Not only did I forget to wear my safety harness, but I forgot to put on the belt for my pants getting up that morning. This was going to have serious consequences. As I was climbing up with my two hands raised above my head to grab the rungs of the ladder, I could feel my pants slipping down around my hips. Having only two hands, and being very high up, I had to grab the ladder with one hand and pull up my pants with the other hand. I had to alternate each hand between grabbing the ladder and pulling up my pants. About three quarter way up the spire, my pants dropped down around my ankles. I shouted to the foreman, who was below me on the ladder, to climb into the nearest deck of flooring. But by then I had another problem! My pants were down around my ankles. My two legs were tied together. I could not get off the ladder. I managed to kick one leg out of the pants, and in doing so, my shoe fell off and fell on the head of the foreman on the ladder below me. Fortunately, he was wearing his safety helmet! I managed to get on to the floor decking and pull up my pants. Now I was worried that maybe one of the local television stations might have pictured my exposed rear end on camera. The local television stations were on hand each day to get pictures for the local news. Fortunately, they were not around at that time. The foreman, who was with me, was not a Catholic, and, in fact, he had never met a Catholic priest until he met me. I could not resist the urge to tell him way up there so high, that not only had he met a Catholic priest, but he also got to see a priest's exposed rear end, and mine was no different from his, except that shamrocks appear on mine on St. Patrick's Day.

98

WORKERS WHISTLE AT NUN

THE SCAFFOLDING AROUND THE CATHEDRAL WAS ERECTED BY a group of Mexicans, who spoke only in Spanish. The only way to communicate with them was through an interpreter by the name of Angel. Because Angel spoke broken English with a very strong accent and I spoke with a strong Irish brogue, there was plenty of misunderstandings between us. Right next to the Cathedral is St. Vincent's Academy. This is a high school (secondary) for girls. It is staffed by The Sisters of Mercy and lay teachers. Most of the sisters no longer wear their religious habit. One particular sister was a very liberated woman. She was young and always dressed very fancy.

When the scaffolding for the Cathedral was being erected next to the school, the Mexican men were admiring the girls. The sister mentioned above phoned me one morning to complain about the Mexicans whistling at the girls. I told her that I would think that the girls would not mind. Just let it be. The Mexicans will be gone in a few days. Some days later, when the scaffolding was level with the second floor of the school, the good sister phoned me again to complain that the Mexicans were looking in the windows at the girls going to the toilet. I responded by telling her to put a sheet across the windows. She was not happy about this solution. Some days later she phoned me, but this time she was very angry. She was upset because the Mexicans were whistling at her! I was highly amused at this and told her she should feel good about that! This really annoyed her. I told her that if she wore her religious habit that the Mexicans, who were all Catholic would be blessing themselves and bowing to her every time she passed by. She hung up the phone on me. I never heard another word from her about the Mexicans.

It should be noted here that every morning before the Mexicans got on the scaffolding, they huddled together and prayed. They did the same at the end of their workday.

99

TRAPPED IN THE CATHEDRAL ATTIC

THE SIXTY-SIX FOOT HIGH VAULTED PLASTER CEILING IN THE cathedral is suspended from the iron rafters of the roof. Access to the attic is by way of a trap door on the outside of the roof. The door opens from the outside only. Access to the trap door is by way of stairs in one of the two steeples. The interior cathedral lights are recessed into the ceiling. They are accessed by standing on catwalks inside the attic. The catwalks are very narrow. To step off a catwalk would result in falling through the plaster ceiling. The attic has a separate lighting system. During the cathedral restoration the old light fixtures were replaced. When they were removed, they left open holes in the ceiling. During this time, there was also repair work taking place on rusted sections of the iron rafters. I was away for a few days. When I returned late one night, I was anxious to inspect work done during my absence. I climbed up the stairwell of the steeple and went out on to the roof to open the trap door to the attic. It was a very windy night. After opening the trap door, I crawled into the attic, leaving the door open. When turning on the attic lights, the door was slammed shut by the wind. Because the door could not be opened from the inside, I was now trapped in the attic. I did not have a mobile phone at that time to contact someone to come and open the door from the outside.

There was nothing I could do about it. I had to spend the night in the attic. I laid down on the narrow catwalk resigned to the fact that this would be my bed for the night. But I was afraid to go to sleep in case I would roll off the catwalk and go right through the plaster ceiling all the way sixty-six feet down to the floor of the cathedral. I also had another concern. What would I do if I got a call from nature during the night! Eventually I dozed off, but woke several times during the night.

Next morning, I heard the workers arriving in the cathedral below. I put my face against one of the holes from where a light fixture was removed. I shouted out in a very loud voice, "HELP, HELP!" The workers, hearing a voice from on high, got a fright and ran out of the cathedral. What seemed like an eternity passed until a few brave souls returned and looked up to figure out where the voice was coming from. I kept calling out for someone to come and get me out of the attic. Eventually, I was rescued. I went straight to a toilet. Responding to the call of nature never felt so good!

100

AT GUN POINT IN CATHEDRAL

AT 8:45 ON THE MORNING OF TUESDAY, OCTOBER 7, 2003, I was at my desk in my office. I heard a woman screaming that there was a man in the Cathedral setting fire to it, and he had a gun.

The Cathedral is linked to the Cathedral House, and the entrance to the Cathedral sacristy is very close to my office door on the second floor. The other Cathedral offices are on the ground floor along with the lower level of the Cathedral. Hearing the woman screaming, I went to my office door and saw that it was Peggy Baker, who was one of the seven full-time Cathedral employees. She was the receptionist at a desk located inside the main entrance to the Cathedral. Her duty was to welcome the hundreds of daily visitors to the Cathedral, who are given guided tours each day by volunteer tour guides or docents.

When Peggy Baker entered the Cathedral that morning from the Cathedral Rectory to go to her desk, she saw a man pouring lighter fluid on the Bishop's Chair (Cathedra). She also saw that the hand-carved pulpit was on fire. The man had a gun in his hand. She immediately returned to the Rectory, screaming and terrified. That was when I met her at the door to the Cathedral Sacristy. I told her to go downstairs and phone the police and fire department. I ran out into the Cathedral and went straight to the Bishop's Chair and removed the burning cushions and threw them on the marble floor. The pulpit was already blazing and there was nothing I could do about that. Just after I removed the burning cushions from the Bishop's Chair, a man appeared from one of the side altars pointing a gun at me.

Having just completed the almost twelve million dollar restoration project a short time before this, and to witness the burning pulpit and Bishop's Chair, to say that I was extremely angry was to put it very mildly! I was raging and had lost any sense of fear. When the man approached me with the gun, I used a litany of vulgar words telling him to drop the ****** gun or I would strangle him and knock his ****** head off. Seeing that I was dressed as a priest and hearing the foul language coming from my priestly mouth, the man looked stunned, as if he could not believe what he was hearing. He looked as if he had become paralyzed by my words. He stood there with his mouth open and still pointing the gun at me. I admit that it was not very priestly of me to use such vulgar language, but I believe it saved my life. If I was polite to him, I know he would have shot me. At this point, I had to restrain myself from taking the gun from him and blowing his brains out!

The Cathedral was now filling up with smoke. I could hear the police and fire sirens outside, so I knew that help was on the way. But I was taking no chances with the armed man. Looking down the barrel of a loaded gun is not a pleasant experience. I wanted the gunman to know that if he made any move that I would go for his gun. So I continued my litany of foul language and completely neutralized him. We stood facing each other for what appeared to be an eternity.

Eventually, the police appeared from behind the high altar with guns drawn. I could not understand why they were just standing there with guns pointed toward him. I asked them to shoot him. When nothing was happening, I told the policeman standing next to me to shoot him. He told me that he could not do that. I asked him to give me his gun and that I would shoot him myself. Another policeman shouted at me to let them handle the situation. To which I pleaded with them to do something, because, by now, the fire was raging, and the Cathedral was filling up with smoke. Because the man had a loaded gun the police did not allow the fire department to come in to put out the fire. Then I started telling the police that they were a bunch of cowards. Eventually, they made their move and tackled the man and had him on the ground. When they put handcuffs on him, I made an attempt to punch him in the face. To prevent me from doing this the police then placed handcuffs on me! Afterwards, they told me they did this to protect me because they were concerned that I would hurt the gunman, and then I would be in trouble.

The gunman was arrested and taken to the police station for interrogation. He admitted the crime, claiming that he had a problem with organized religion and wanted to make a statement.

He indicated that he had come from Atlanta on the previous day and took one of the city tours. He discovered that the Cathedral was the largest church in Georgia, and so this became his perfect target. He also indicated that he had three plans which were: a nighttime attack, a daytime attack, or take the priest hostage. Since he was unable to enter the church at night, he carried out the daytime attack. Finding out where he had stayed the previous night, the police searched his room and found receipts for the purchase of lighter fluid and a cigarette lighter. The receipt indicated the location of the store where he purchased the lighter fluid and cigarette lighter. They went to this store and confiscated the closed circuit video, which showed the gunman taking the items from the shelves in the store and checking them out. He was charged with arson and aggravated assault and being in possession of a gun in the church. He was sent to prison and ordered to appear in court on a specific date sometime later.

In court he had a public defender represent him. I was called to the witness box to give my testimony. The public defender stated that I intimidated his client. This annoyed me. I replied that if I was nice to him, he would have shot me, and that if the public defender was not more careful about what he was saying that I could intimidate him too! At that point, there was laughter from the public gallery, and the judge had to call for order in court. I was then asked if I had a conversation with the accused. I turned toward the judge, saying, "I did." Then I asked him if I had his permission to quote the exact words of my conversation because I wanted to tell the whole truth and nothing but the whole truth. Guessing what I had said to the accused, the judge stated that would not be necessary! The gunman was convicted of arson and aggravated assault and was sentenced to twenty years in prison. After imposing sentence, the judge told the gunman that he was lucky that the police rescued him from the priest!

The total cost for the clean up and other repairs and

replacement of the pulpit was almost a half-million dollars. During the clean-up in the area where the gunman confronted me, an empty shell casing was found. We do know that five live bullets were found in the gun, and one bullet had been fired. I have absolutely no recollection of a shot being fired, but the empty shell-casing being found in the area where I confronted the gunman and that fact that there were five live bullets in the gun and one fired, would indicate that he did fire a shot. The name of the gunman was Stuart Vincent Smith. He was 31 years of age.

101

THE OLD TRUMPET PLAYER

SAVANNAH, GEORGIA, IS THE SIXTH MOST VISITED CITY IN America. River Street attracts many tourists. I often take a walk along River Street dressed as a priest. It gives me an opportunity to meet and talk with people. Many of them have never met or talked with a priest. On one of my walks along River Street, I came across an old African American man playing a trumpet. His trumpet was also old and battered. I stood to one side and listened to this man play beautiful jazz music. When he finished his tune, I approached him and asked him if he could play "Danny Boy." He seemed pleased that I asked him, and then he put the trumpet to his lips and played the most beautiful rendition I ever heard of "Danny Boy."

When he finished playing, I put a few coins in his cardboard box. He thanked me. Then he bent down and picked up one of the coins and gave it to me saying, "Reverend, please give this to your church for me." I was so touched by his generosity that I took out my wallet and gave him a twenty-dollar bill. Whenever the Sunday Gospel tells the story of The Widow's Mite, I always begin my sermon by telling my story about the generosity of the old African American trumpet player on River Street in Savannah, Georgia.

102

THE THREE WISE MEN

ON THE NIGHT BEFORE THE FEAST OF THE EPIPHANY 2016, I had an interesting experience. Around 10:00 p.m., I decided to take a short walk around the outside of the Cathedral before going to bed. As I walked by the front of the Cathedral, I saw three men standing at one of the front doors, which were locked. It was obvious to me that they were homeless men. I was wearing my collar, and I stopped to chat with them. They wanted to know if they could go inside to see the Baby Jesus in the crib. I am sure that they were not interested in the Baby Jesus! They more than likely wanted to find a spot where they could sleep for the night. Because it was the eve of The Epiphany, they reminded me of The Three Wise Men looking for the Baby Jesus.

I told them I would take them inside for a look. The priests' house, where I live, and the Cathedral offices are attached to the back of the Cathedral. I brought them around and into the house and out into the Cathedral. From the way they acted on entering the majestic interior of the Cathedral I could figure

253

out that they were not Catholic. Our Christmas Nativity scene, or crib, is very large and takes a few weeks to assemble. It has all sorts of things in it, including waterfalls with running water. I turned on the lights in it and the pumps started running and the water was running down the waterfalls. The three men gasped in wonder and awe. In fact, one of them mumbled to himself the words, "Holy ****," which I thought was very funny! The poor fellows! I think they thought they had died and gone into Heaven!

Well, then I took them over close to the part of the crib where the infant is placed in the manger. One of the men got down on his knees and bent over bowing his head. Then the other two did the same thing. Now I had three homeless men on their knees bent over in solemn adoration in front of the statue of the Baby Jesus. My God, I thought to myself, this is what happened when the Three Wise Men found the Infant Jesus in the stable in Bethlehem.

I have been to Bethlehem several times, so I pictured that place in my mind, and I knelt down and bent over and bowed my head with the three homeless men. After this, I brought them to the kitchen and made coffee for them and gave them some bread and sliced meat. We had a great chat. This took over an hour and was long past my bedtime. As they were about to leave, I thought of the Innkeeper in Bethlehem, who did not have a place for the Holy Family. So I put the three homeless men into my car and took them to a city shelter for the homeless where they could spend the night.

103

A HOLY COMMUNION VISIT

AN ELDERLY WOMAN LIVED WITH HER DIVORCED SON. HE
left for work each morning around eight o'clock and returned
home around six o'clock in the evening. The old woman was
very feeble and used a walker to get around her house. Because
she was alone during the day, and was probably lonely and
starved for conversation, I took her Holy Communion on
Thursday of each week. We had an arrangement that I would
arrive at two o'clock, and she would have the front door
unlocked and spare herself the effort of walking to the door.

When I arrived one Thursday the door was locked. There
was no response when I rang the doorbell and banged on the
door. I went around to the back door and got no response. I
noticed her bedroom window was open. I went to the window
and called out her name. She replied that she was in bed. I
asked her to come to the window, and I would give her Holy
Communion. She replied that she was unable to get out of bed.
I was determined to go in and make sure that she did not have a
stroke or needed medical attention. The small window of her

bathroom was open and right underneath it was an air conditioner condenser. I stepped up on the unit and climbed in the window. I stepped on to the toilet bowl. When I entered the bedroom, the old woman was sitting on the edge of the bed. I said, "You told me you could not get out of bed." She replied, "I got affright, thinking a burglar was coming in the window." I wondered if I would have to give her another fright to get her back into the bed.

I gave her Holy Communion and spent some time talking with her. I helped her back into bed and asked her where the key to the door was so that I could let myself out. She had no idea where the key was, and I worried about her being trapped in a locked house. She assured me that she would be fine and that her son would be home around six and he would find the key. Because I was unable to leave through the door, the only way out was the way I came in through the bathroom window. I stepped up on the toilet bowl, and as I looked out the window, I saw two police officers with guns drawn. They ordered me to come out. When I came out, they handcuffed me and charged me with burglary! When I explained the reason for being in the house, one of them climbed in the window to verify my explanation. He returned with a big smile on his face and apologized. It seems that a neighbor, who saw me go in through the window, alerted the police. The two police officers were not Catholic and humbly begged my forgiveness. I replied in Latin, "Ego te absolvo." Not understanding what I said, one of them replied, "We think it was funny too."

104

THE OLD WOMAN'S BED

I took Holy Communion to the home of a ninety-two year old woman. She lived with her seventy-year-old daughter who was a widow. The old woman was confined to bed. Her bad was a large king size. The old woman, who was very frail, was lying in the very middle of the bed. When reaching in to give her Holy Communion, I had to place my left hand on the bed to maintain my balance while placing the Sacred Host on her tongue with my right hand. I was often tempted to kneel up on the bed to get close to her!

On one occasion, while leaning over the bed to give her Holy Communion, my body somehow caused the bed to collapse! Because I was leaning on the bed with my left hand, I fell in on the bed when it collapsed. I was on top of the old woman, who had rolled out toward the edge of the tilted bed. I was slightly shocked being in this unpredicted position. The Sacred Host had fallen out of my right hand and got lost somewhere in the bed. I apologized for the mishap. But I became amused when the old woman giggled and said, "Monsignor, you are in bed with me!" I replied, "I am, and we have Jesus with us." Her daughter, who was in the room, came to help me get off the bed. Because she was concerned about her mother being rolled over and wedged against the frame of the bed, she asked me to help her out of the bed. I replied that I had to find Jesus first! After I found the Sacred Host, I placed it back into the container (pyx) and helped to get the old woman out of the bed. We sat her on a chair and got the bed fixed up.

I gave the old woman Holy Communion while she was sitting on the chair. We spent a little while in silence while she said her prayers. I just sat there pondering what had happened. The old woman looked so frail. She was just a bundle of bones. I kept thinking that I could have crushed her when I fell on top of her in the bed. After a period of silence, the old woman was the first to speak. She was a good sport. She started giggling and put her hands to her face and said, "When one lives long enough, life can be full of surprises. I never in my life imagined a priest falling into bed with me." We all had a great laugh and speculated on how I should give Holy Communion to the old woman on future visits.

105

THE BLONDE AT THE BAR

Every Saturday night after the evening Mass at the cathedral, for the past several years I go to The Sixpence Pub for my dinner. This is a five-minute walk from the cathedral. As a regular customer for many years, I am well known to the staff. They do not give me a menu because they know what I want to eat. My order is always a pint of Bass ale and a pot roast. This is a British pub and a very popular restaurant with the many tourists, who visit Savannah. They do not take reservations there so seating is on a first-come first-serve basis. Because it is usually crowded, when a group of people go there to eat, they must wait until their name is called to get a table. Meals are also served at the bar counter. Going there on your own has the advantage of finding an empty seat at the bar upon arrival.

Upon arrival one particular Saturday evening, I took a seat on an empty high stool at the bar. I was dressed casually. Sitting next to me was a blonde, sitting alone having a glass of wine. We exchanged smiles and some small talk. As soon as I took my seat at the bar and without saying a word to the barmaid, she placed a pint of Bass ale on the counter in front of me, saying that she will give me my dinner in a little while. The blonde, noticing that I was served without placing an order, looked at me and said, "You must come here often; they seem to know you." I replied, "I am the owner." "My, oh my," she replied. Then I told her that I was only joking and that I was a regular customer and the staff know what I want. With Savannah being the sixth most visited city in the USA, I asked her if she was visiting here. She told me that she drove up from Jacksonville, Florida, to visit her daughter who was a student at The Savannah College of Art & Design, known here as SCAD. She then went on to tell me that her daughter was out that evening and that she came out for a quiet evening and a glass of wine. I replied that I came out for my dinner and a nice quiet evening too. Then I asked her where she was staying. She informed me that she was staying just down the street. With a smile, I told her that I was staying just down the street too! By now, the blonde was all smiles and was probably expecting me to escort her home.

Just at that moment, a parishioner and his wife, who had been to the Saturday evening Mass at the cathedral, came up to me and complimented me on the excellent homily I had given at Mass that evening. The blonde seemed startled by this comment. After some conversation, the couple left and the blonde asked me if I am a priest? When I told her that I am, she seemed confused and asked me why I did not tell her that. "Well, you did not ask me," I replied. Then there was a brief period of silence while she was trying to absorb what I had just told her.

Then she informed me that she was a Baptist and had never met a Catholic priest. She went on to say that she came out for a nice quiet evening and did not expect to meet a Catholic priest sitting at a bar drinking beer. Because Baptists do not drink alcohol, I replied that I came out for a nice quiet evening to prepare my sermon, and that I did not expect to meet a good Baptist lady sitting at a bar drinking wine! This amused her. After a brief pause, she went on to tell me that she had not been to church in several years. I looked at her and smiled and placed my hand on her hand and told her that she was my kind of woman! She was startled by this remark. To assure her that I had no ulterior motive for my remark, I told her that what I meant by that was that people like her kept me in business, and that by not going to church did not make her a bad person. I then told her that she was a good person and that God loves her. By now she seemed ready to confide in me. She went on to tell me that she left the Baptist church because she was harshly reprimanded by her minister over what she considered a trivial matter. I told her that she should not abandon her church just because of a bad experience with one minister. I encouraged her to find another Baptist church. She insisted that she had no further interest in attending any church. She then went on to tell me that she had never been inside a Catholic Church. I invited her to come to the ten o'clock Mass next morning at the cathedral just for a new experience. I told her that I would be celebrating that Mass, and I would make sure she felt comfortable and at peace there. She agreed to give it a try. We chatted a little more before I went home. Before leaving, I assured her she would be very welcome next morning at the cathedral, and that I would be very disappointed if she did not come. She promised me that she would be there.

Next morning, Sunday, I was at the entrance to the cathedral, greeting people as they arrived, as is our custom. Sure enough, there was the blonde dressed like a film star, making her way up the many steps to the cathedral door. She approached me with a big smile and gave me a very affectionate hug. I told her how happy I was to see her and instructed her to take a seat in the very front pew underneath the pulpit. I directed one of the ushers to escort her to the front pew under the pulpit. As the entrance procession approached the altar railing to the sound of music from the massive pipe organ and the choir and congregation singing, I stepped aside to the pew where the blonde was standing. I assured her of how glad I was that she came, and to make her feel at ease, as it was her first time inside a Catholic Church and among a congregation of total strangers. I am sure the Catholic liturgy was very strange to her with all the kneeling, standing, and sitting.

When it came time for me to deliver my sermon, I stood in the pulpit and looked out over the full church of approximately one thousand souls. I took a deep breath and paused before saying a word. A preacher must get the attention of his congregation before he can start preaching. This morning I knew how I would get their attention. I solemnly announced that before giving my homily, I had something to tell them about myself. I told them, "I want to tell you about the blonde in my life!" Well, that did get their attention. I told them about the good Baptist lady, who I met at The Sixpence Pub the previous evening, who had never been inside a Catholic Church, and that I had invited her to attend Mass that morning. The blonde was enjoying all this attention. I informed the congregation that she was sitting in the front pew underneath the pulpit. I asked her to stand up and invited the congregation to show their welcome to her with a round of applause. The blonde stood up and beamed all over as the congregation applauded her. I could tell that she loved all the attention given to her by a church full of strangers. When the applauding stopped, she sat down and took out her handkerchief and dried her eyes. She was obviously touched by all this attention. At the end of Mass, we processed down the center aisle to the entrance. On the way, I stopped at her pew and asked her what she thought of the service. With tears in her eyes, she replied that she could stay there forever! It reminded me of the Gospel story of Peter, James, and John at the transfiguration of Christ on Mount Tabor! I told her I would be outside the church to greet people as they were leaving, and I would be waiting for her.

I greeted the long line of people as they came out from Mass. At the end of the line was the blonde. She told me that she never had such a pleasant experience in church and was overwhelmed by the welcome she received. She added that she never before felt so close to God and asked what she had to do to become a Catholic. I advised her to take her time about that and give it some time as her emotions were now taking over. Then she said that she would like to find out more about the Catholic Church. I gave her the name of a priest friend of mine from college in Ireland and the name of his church in Jacksonville. I suggested that she contact him for advice. I gave her my calling card with my name and contact information and asked her to keep in touch with me.

Several weeks later she contacted me to let me know that she had several meetings with my priest friend in Jacksonville, and that she had signed up to take the next session of convert classes at the church. When the classes started, she called me on a regular basis to let me know how much she enjoyed it and had made up her mind to become a Catholic. She was received into the Catholic Church at the Easter Vigil of that year.

About a year later, she called me to let me know that her husband, who never attended church, had expressed an interest in the Catholic Church. He had signed up to take the convert classes. He was so inspired by the blonde's happiness at being a Catholic that he decided to do likewise. Now, some years later, they are both very active at their church. They are both Lectors and Ministers of Holy Communion. It is amazing how God works! And all this began at the counter of a pub with a Catholic priest drinking beer and a Baptist lady drinking wine!

106

WEDDING COUPLE LIED

AT THE CATHEDRAL IN SAVANNAH WE GET MANY REQUESTS for weddings. In order to have available dates for parishioners, wedding ceremonies are limited to parishioners, or to those who have a family connection with the cathedral, to those who live in the Diocese of Savannah. A lady, who claimed to be a parishioner, phoned me to arrange a wedding at the cathedral. After asking her a few questions, I began to suspect that she was not a parishioner. I became convinced that she was not after I asked her what particular Sunday Mass she usually attended and if I had ever spoken to her after Mass. She hesitated and made a bad mistake by stating that she attended a Mass time, which we did not have. I knew then that she was not a parishioner, and if she was, she did not ever attend Mass. I decided to play along with her and set up a date and time for her and her fiancée to meet with me.

On the evening we were to meet, I went outside the house a few minutes ahead of their arrival time. I was not dressed as a priest. When I saw a couple get out of a car and start walking toward me holding hands, I suspected this had to be them. I had never seen either one of them before. I started walking toward them. They walked past me without saying a word. Obviously, they had no idea who I was! Then I stopped and waited until they got to the door of the house.

I could see that they were getting annoyed when nobody was answering the doorbell. Then I walked back toward the door and asked them if I could help them. The lady replied that they had an appointment arranged with Monsignor O'Neill. I asked them if they were sure that their appointment was for that particular evening. She replied that it was. I said that was strange because Monsignor O'Neill was away for a few days and was surprised that he did not contact them to cancel the appointment. By now, they were really annoyed that the Monsignor did not contact them to cancel the appointment. I asked if they knew the Monsignor and if he knew them. She replied that they knew him very well. I was enjoying all this as they kept digging the hole deeper. They had no idea who I was. I suggested that they go home and call the Monsignor in a few days and make another appointment and be sure to let him know what they thought of him for not contacting them to change the appointment. When they started to walk away, I told them I was a priest, who happened to be visiting, and asked if there was anything I could do to help. They told me that they were to meet with the Monsignor to fill out papers for a wedding. I replied that I think I could do that for them if I could find the papers. I invited them into my office. I sat behind my desk and they sat opposite me. They were still very annoyed that the Monsignor did not cancel the meeting. I asked them for their names and if they were parishioners and how well they knew the Monsignor and how well he knew them. They assured me that they were parishioners and knew Monsignor O'Neill very well and that he knew them very well. By now it was time for me to give them the surprise of their life!

I told them I had to go to another room to see if I could find the papers needed to be completed for the wedding. I left the office and returned about five minutes later. When I entered the office, I introduced myself as being Monsignor O'Neill. They were stunned. I thought they would wet their underwear with the shock. I sat down behind my desk and gave them a lecture for telling lies and trying to pull a fast one on me. I asked each of them if they had ever been married before. When they replied that they had not, I told them that I could not believe anything they told me since they had already lied to me. I went on to say that there was no point in completing the papers because I could not believe anything they would tell me. The girl started crying, telling me she was really sorry and wanted to get married at the Cathedral and took a chance telling me she was a parishioner. We did not complete any wedding papers that evening. Instead, we talked at length about the importance of telling the truth. I told them that if they had told the truth to begin with, when I met them at the door, that I would probably have found a soft spot in my heart to officiate at their wedding at the Cathedral. I pointed out that if I had answered the door when they arrived, they would have guessed who I was. But by my meeting them on the street and they did not know who, their plan to deceive me was spoiled. After some further conversation on the importance of telling the truth, I believed they had learned a lesson and were truly contrite. We arranged another time and date to complete the paper work. Several months later I officiated at their wedding. As the years went by, I baptized their children, and we became great friends.

107

SARAH, DON'T LEAVE ME!

I MISPLACED MY CREDIT CARD AND HAD IT CANCELLED. A new credit card was issued. There was one automatic payment from my card due each month. I had to phone this company to give my new credit card number. This can be an undertaking requiring much patience. On placing a phone call, one has to listen to a menu and go through several steps before finding a real human person at the other end of the line. Finally, on getting a person a series of questions were asked. When asked for the number of my cancelled card, I did not know what it was. Then I was asked to stay on the line while being transferred to another person. In the course of the transfer, and while being placed on hold, the phone got disconnected. I had to start it all over again and go through the same annoying process.

Having gone through this annoying process twice, my patience had worn out. On the third attempt when I finally got a person to respond, it was a very pleasant lady. She greeted me saying, "Hello, my name is Sarah. How can I help you?" I began by telling her that I had run out of patience because this was my third attempt to get my problem solved. I also told her to be prepared because I was liable to use some words she may not like to hear. She assured me that would not be a problem. Sarah then asked me the usual questions. We were doing fine until she asked me for my old credit card number. When I did not have it, she said she had to put me on hold and transfer me to another person. I passionately pleaded with her saying: "Sarah, don't leave me! Sarah, Sarah, please don't leave me." She replied that she was unable to help me and had to put me on hold and transfer my call to another person. I told her I could not deal any further with this. Just before she went to place me on hold, it dawned on me where I might be able to find my old number. So I asked her to hold on so that I could make a search. I found it and got back to her with the information. Sarah was then able to complete the transaction, and I assured her of my appreciation for being so kind and patient with me.

Later in the evening of that day, I was having dinner with Sister Rose Mary Collins in a restaurant. I was telling her about my troubles with the phone calls to sort out my credit card problem. When I got to the part about my conversation with Sarah, I got really excited and was speaking louder than I realized. I was unaware that people sitting at nearby tables were listening and watching me. I was so excited, when I got to relating my pleading with Sarah not to leave me, I was using my hands passionately saying to Sister Rose Mary, "Sarah, don't leave me! Please Sarah, don't leave me!" Sister Rose Mary was in stitches laughing at me. A lady at the next table, thinking that Sister Rose Mary was Sarah, got up and came over to reprimand her. She pointed her finger at Sister Rose Mary and told her to have compassion and be kind to that dear sweet man, who was hurting very much. We explained to this woman that Sister Rose Marry was not Sarah. I explained that I was relating a story about a phone conversation with a person named Sarah. The woman was relieved to know this, and we saw the funny side of the story. From that point on, Sister Rose Mary referred to herself as Sarah!

108

MEET ME AT THE CEMETERY

THIS STORY IS SIMILAR TO A PREVIOUS STORY. IT IS ANOTHER story about an abusive man. This happened in Savannah. There was a woman, who was taking the weekly convert classes. These classes are for people who are not Catholic but are interested in becoming Catholic or finding out more about the Catholic Church. Catholics also attend to learn more about the teachings of the church. This woman arrived for class one evening with her face badly bruised. I asked her if she was in an accident. She informed me that her boyfriend beat her. I asked her to remain after class so that I could talk with her. It turned out that her boyfriend was living with her and that he had a few guns in the house. I also found out that he had been in a few other live-in relationships with a similar record. She had not informed the police because she was afraid of what he might do to her. He had no religion, did not attend any church, and was angry with her for taking the convert classes at a Catholic Church. I got her permission to phone him and arrange a meeting with him.

When I phoned him and asked him to come and talk with me, he used profane words saying that he would never set foot on the grounds of a Catholic Church. Knowing that he had guns, I did not feel safe going to his house. A very short distance from the cathedral there is an old historical cemetery, which no longer has burials. It is called Colonial Cemetery. Since the man did not want to come to the cathedral, and I did not want to go to his house, I suggested to him that we meet in neutral grounds. I suggested that we meet at Colonial Cemetery. He agreed. There are a few entrances to the cemetery. Since we had never met, I told him that I would meet him at the main entrance gate, which had an eagle over the archway. I told him that I would be dressed as a priest so that he could easily identify me. He arrived at the appointed time. He looked like a real gangster that I would not want to get into a fight with. He was also a big man. But I was determined to act like a gangster myself! I invited the man to walk with me to an area in the cemetery where duels were fought over one hundred years ago. It is a concrete paved area with some concrete seating. On arrival there, I told him that duels were fought there in the past and that maybe we might have a duel there that day. This got his attention. I asked him if he had a gun with him. He showed me a pistol he had in his pocket. I told him that did not bother me, and that I almost strangled a man with a gun, who tried to burn down the cathedral. Then I tricked him by pretending that I had a few friends with guns hiding in bushes in the cemetery. If we got into a fight, they would come and blow his brains out. He was looking at me with amazement!

Having finished my words of introduction, I went on to discuss his relationship with the lady, who was taking the convert classes at the cathedral. He was very defensive and made it clear that he had strong objections to her taking classes in religion. To make a long story short, we were getting nowhere. We had also discussed his previous relationships with the other women he had lived with. I told him that he was an abuser of women, and because of his track record, he should not be with any woman. Because they were not married and only living together, I told him that I was going to give him twenty-four hours to go home and pack his bags and vanish. If he did not do this, I would have my friends abduct him, and he would never be heard from or seen again. I was amazed that he took me seriously on this! He promised me that he would go straight home and get his few earthly possessions and leave the city of Savannah. I told him to do that because my friends in the bushes were going to follow him at a distance and keep a watchful eye on him. I could not believe that this very big gangster-looking man with a gun on him became so docile and was willing to do whatever I demanded. As he left the cemetery, I told him that my friends were watching and ready to abduct him if he was not gone by twenty-four hours. He walked away like a very frightened man. My bluff about my imaginary friends in the bushes worked!

The following week the woman was back for class. When the class ended she stayed behind, and we had a long chat. She told me that he came home trembling. He asked her if every Catholic priest was like that priest at the cathedral. He told her that he was never so afraid because I had men hiding in bushes at the cemetery, who were waiting to attack him. He told her he was leaving the city immediately and had no idea where he was going to go. He left in a hurry with his collection of guns and a few odds and ends. She was a happy woman that he was gone from her life. The following Easter she became a Catholic.

Sometime later she met a nice man who took the convert classes and became a Catholic. I officiated at their wedding. They no longer live in Savannah, but I am in regular contact with them. There has been no trace or sign of the gangster-looking man with the gun that I met at the cemetery!

109

THE ONION WOMAN

My encounter with the woman who I refer to as "The Onion Woman," is one of my more memorable experiences as a priest. I had to make a sick-call to a man who had cancer. He lived about forty miles out from Savannah in rural Georgia. There was no Catholic Church in his locality. I got a phone call from the sick man's wife asking me to come to the house and anoint him and bring him Holy Communion. She gave me the address, which had a mail box number located on Old Mill Creek Road. She gave me directions which eventually would take me off the Interstate Highway and on to a very rural road. I was to travel along this road for a few miles until I reached a small church and cemetery. Then I had to take another rural road until I came to another church and a garage.

On a day I arranged to visit the sick man, I drove following directions until I reached the little church and garage. There I could get directions to Old Mill Creek Road. When I arrived at the garage, I got out of my car to ask for directions. There are very few if any Catholics in this area. I was met by a young lady wearing a cowboy hat and cowboy boots. She looked very surprised to see me because I was dressed as a priest. It was probably the first time in her life that she met a priest! With a very typical rural Georgia accent and speaking in a local dialect, she asked if she could help me. I told her I was looking for directions to Old Mill Creek Road. She replied that she had no idea where it was, but she would ask the mechanic in the garage if he could help. The mechanic, who had very greasy hands and a shaggy beard, came out. He had no idea either. He told me that if I went on by the side of the little church and kept going "yonder" for a few miles I might find it in that area.

At this point I thought the best thing to do, was to phone the wife of the sick man to come get me at the garage. When I went to phone her, my mobile phone was not getting any signal. I was really out in the middle of nowhere. I drove off and went a few miles yonder as instructed by the garage mechanic. Along the way, which was a very narrow road, there was nothing but pine trees on both sides. There was not a house in sight. Eventually, I came upon a very small cabin, which was set back in the trees. Outside of the cabin there was an old pick-up truck, which badly needed a coat of paint. There was a lady sitting in the truck behind the steering wheel.

Standing next to the driver's window and speaking to the lady behind the steering wheel, was a very overweight and voluptuous woman. I stopped and let down the window of my car. I asked her for directions to Old Mill Creek Road. She walked toward me chewing tobacco. She turned her head to one side and shot out a massive big spit. The spit was so big that she could have shot down a bird! She had no idea where Old Mill Creek Road was but told me to continue on for another mile to a country store and I might be able to get help there. I was fascinated by this woman and her spitting chewing tobacco. I thought to myself that she could have an interesting story to tell about her life. I drove off thinking that I must come back later and chat with her. When I arrived at the country store, there were several pickup trucks parked there. Most of the drivers were women wearing cowboy hats and cowboy boots. Being dressed as a priest in this locality, which had no Catholics, I decided not to get out to ask for directions. As I was about to head back home and give up on finding Old Mill Creek Road, I checked my phone and was delighted to find that I now had a signal. I phoned the sick man's wife and told her where I was and asked her to come and get me. I could follow her to her house.

She arrived about ten minutes later in a pickup truck. I followed her to her house. There was no way that I could have found it on my own. It was about three miles away. To get to it we took three different side roads from the main road. The side roads where not paved. The surface was just clay. Being summer time, the dust from the pickup truck I was following made it difficult for me to see where I was going. I can only imagine what it must be like to drive on those roads when it rains.

On arrival at the house, I anointed the sick man and gave him Holy Communion. His wife kept horses as pets. To give the sick man time to be alone to say his prayers, his wife took me outside to see the horses. I told her about my father and how he got rid of the tinker's horses when they were secretly grazing in our fields during the night. Having grown up with farm horses in Ireland, we spent some time having what one could call "horse-talk." After this, we went back into the house so that I could visit with the sick man. I was telling him about the trouble I had getting directions to his place. I told him about the various people I met when looking for directions. When I told him about the girl at the garage with the cowboy hat, he told me that they are very cautious about strangers there, and that I was lucky she did not appear with a shotgun in her hands. Then I went on to tell him about the overweight woman chewing tobacco and her massive big spit. I told him that I found her to be a person of interest and that on my way home I planned to stop at her house and have a chat with her. He strongly advised me to keep going because I was a stranger. After a nice visit with the man and his wife, I left. As I drove back along the unpaved roads to the main road, I decided to ignore the advice of the sick man about my intention to stop and visit the overweight woman. I really wanted to talk with her because I was certain that she had a story to tell.

When I arrived at the overweight woman's cabin, the pickup truck was gone. The woman was sitting on a swing seat on her front porch. When I got out of my car she said, "Preacher man, did you find the place you were looking for?" I replied that I did, and that I was stopping to thank her for helping me. She did not believe this. She said I was stopping to get her to come to church. I assured her that was not so. She then said that she had no time for preachers and had no interest in a church. Then she asked me what religion I practiced. When I told her that I was Catholic, she told me that they were all going to hell. Then she said that most preachers look angry and shout at people from their pulpits. I used a bit of blarney on her and told her that God loved her and agreed with her that most preachers were not friendly. She picked up on this and complimented me for being friendly and smiling at her. She invited me to come over and sit next to her. I sat on what was a rickety old rocking chair. As soon as I sat down, I noticed a double-barrel shotgun leaning against the wall behind her. I pretended not to notice it. If I mentioned it, she would probably want to show me how she fired it. We had some small talk for a little while. But I was anxious to get the story of her life. I asked her about her family.

She had a husband, who was the father of the girl I saw earlier in the pick-up truck. That girl was now living in South Carolina. The overweight woman was getting ready to go and live with her daughter. She went on to tell me that her husband left her many years ago, and she had no idea where he was or if he was dead or alive. She lived on her own for a few years with her one child. Times got hard for her, and she worked at two jobs. She met a man, who was a lumberjack, working in the many pine forests in the area. Eventually, they formed a relationship, and he came to live with her. She was glad to have his financial assistance. But there was one big problem. The lumberjack could not get enough sex, and she was exhausted from him. But then things got worse when she found out that he was also having sex with another woman, whose husband was a truck driver. She found out that when the truck driver was away for a few days, the lumberjack spent the nights with his wife. When the truck driver was home, the lumberjack spent the night with the overweight woman. Looking at this extremely overweight woman and trying to picture her and the lumberjack in bed together, I asked her how long ago all this was. I think she knew what I was getting at! She told me all this was about thirty years ago when she was very slim and sexy looking!

She went on to tell me that one evening, when she knew that the truck driver was home, the lumberjack would spend the night with her, she decided to get even with him and cure his lust. When he came to bed with her that night, she grabbed him by what she referred to as "his onions" and squeezed them as tight as she could. He screamed in agony and while he was getting out of the bed, she held on to his onions and tried to pull them off him. When she lost her grip, he left the bedroom screaming. She never saw him after that. While she was telling me all this, I sat there with my mouth open, and I could actually feel the lumberjack's pain! All this reminded me of the calf at home in Tipperary, mistaking the bull's testicles for the cow's udder! I knew this woman would have a story, but I got more than I expected! After this, I wanted to go home. As I was leaving, she said that she hoped to see me again before she went to live in South Carolina. I promised to return. I was anxious for another story!

Because the sick man referred to earlier in this story was so sick, I promised him that I would bring him Holy Communion once a week, even though the distance was very far. When I made my next visit to him the following week, I told him about my visit with the overweight woman. He was amazed that I did this, in spite of his advice not to do that. However, he really enjoyed the story about her and the lumberjack. We referred to her as 'The Onion Woman.' On my way back from my second visit to the sick man, I called again to visit The Onion Woman. It was the last time I would meet her because she was moving away in a few days to live with her daughter in South Carolina. As I was leaving her, she told me that she was glad that she met me, in spite of the fact that she had no time for preachers. She told me that I had changed her opinion on that, and that when she got settled in South Carolina that she would consider talking with a Catholic priest to find out more about the Catholic Church.

110

MY TRANS-ATLANTIC TELEPHONE

WHEN I LEFT FOR AMERICA IN 1967, AND DURING MY EARLY years there, very few homes in rural Ireland had telephones. Whenever I made a phone call to Ireland, which was no more than once a year, I had to make arrangements in advance by mail with my family. A date and time was arranged for them to be at the house of a neighbor who had a telephone. At that time, there was no such convenience as direct dialing. To make a phone call from America to Ireland, the operator connected with a telephone exchange in Dublin. The Dublin telephone exchange then connected with the telephone exchange in Tipperary town. The telephone exchange in Tipperary town then connected with the telephone exchange in my local village. The telephone exchange in my local village then connected with the home of my neighbor. This process took about twenty minutes to complete. Whenever one of the many connections got lost, the process had to be started all over again! Meanwhile, my family, waiting for the call, was wondering why I was not calling at the arranged time.

In my office, I had a milking machine and a six-gallon milk tankard. The milking machine was on a small table, and the milk tankard was on the floor. They were situated right inside my office door. A parishioner came to my office to discuss some matter. When he saw the milking machine, he asked me what that apparatus was. He had never seen anything like it. With a straight face, I told him that it was an old-time Trans-Atlantic Telephone, which was commonly used in Ireland many years ago, when few people had telephones in their homes. He was absolutely fascinated by this apparatus. He stood over it and carefully inspected it. Then he walked back from it and looked at it from a distance. Then he came back to it and inspected it again. He was absolutely amazed. Then he asked me how it worked. I gave a demonstration by taking the cluster of four milking cups in my hand. They were attached to the lid of the milking bucket by a tube through which the milk flowed from the cow to the bucket. Holding the cluster of four milking cups in my hand, I held one cup to my ear. I told the man to hold another cup to his ear. I explained to him that since the cluster had four milking cups, that four people could listen on the phone at the same time. Then he asked how to speak into the phone. I explained that this was done by taking the milking cup from the ear and placing it by the mouth. He was so excited over all this that he said he had to bring his wife in to see it. I was amazed that this man actually believed me!

Some days later he brought his wife in to see my Trans-Atlantic Telephone. When they entered my office he got very excited explaining to his wife how this phone worked. He took the cluster of milking cups and had his wife hold one cup to her ear. Then he placed a milking cup to his ear. To make the demonstration more clear, I placed another cup by my ear. So now we had three people on the same phone. Then he demonstrated how to talk into the phone. Meanwhile, his wife was rolling her eyes and making faces. She had doubts about all this. It so happened that I had a large picture on the wall behind the milking machine of a cow being milked by a milking machine at home in Tipperary. When the man finished giving his demonstration to his wife, he placed the cluster of milking cups back on the hook on the handle of the bucket. He was still very excited over being able to show his wife how much he knew about old-style Irish Trans-Atlantic Telephones. All this time, his wife was scrutinizing the picture on the wall behind the milking machine of the cow being milked in Tipperary. She looked at me, shaking her head, and asked me if the Trans-Atlantic Telephone and what she could see in the picture were the same thing. With a big grin on my face, I admitted to her that they were. She shook her head and looked at her husband and asked him how could be so stupid to believe that a milking machine could be a telephone. The poor man was so deflated and crushed! He accused me of being an Irish rouge and scoundrel. Then the wife said it was time to take him home before I gave him another outlandish story about the many other items of interest in my office, which I had collected over many years at flea markets and junkyards.

111

A DOG AT A FUNERAL

AS A PRIEST, I HAVE ALWAYS TRIED TO PORTRAY THE HUMAN
face of the Church. There was a man in the Cathedral parish in
Savannah whose parents immigrated to America from Ireland.
He had a son who had a pet greyhound dog. The greyhound's
name was Meave, named after the mythical Irish Queen Meave.
The greyhound was a reject from the dog racing tracks in
Miami, Florida. It was a reject because when chasing the electric hare around the track, it turned back about halfways. In my
opinion, this was a smart dog because it was able to sniff out
that the hare was not real. It was only a piece of metal moving
along on an underground cable.

The man's son was killed in an accident. When he came to
make funeral arrangements for his son, I expressed concern for
the greyhound. This poor dog was going to be very lonely,
following the death of its master. As I saw it, the greyhound
had to be in mourning. As a mourner, the greyhound should be
at the funeral. I insisted that the greyhound should be with the
family in the front pew during the funeral Mass. The man was

285

very touched by this and agreed to bring the greyhound to the funeral.

At the funeral Mass, I began my sermon by offering my sympathy to the family of the deceased young man and to his pet greyhound. I could see it was sad and in mourning. When I finished my sermon, I got down from the pulpit and went to the front pew to express my sympathy to the family and to the greyhound. I patted the greyhound on the head and rubbed its back telling it how sorry I was for its loss. The mournful greyhound seemed to appreciate my words of sympathy. It wagged his tail frantically, which kept banging against the front of the pew. It was actually whining with grief.

After the funeral Mass was over, the coffin was brought out to the plaza steps at the front door of the Cathedral. When the coffin was coming out the door, a bagpiper started playing a haunting Irish lament tune. With the piercing shrill of the bagpipes, the dear, sweet greyhound started wailing and groaning. This broke my heart. I noticed several people started crying. I am sure they sensed the greyhound's pain. When we got to the cemetery, the bagpiper was there. As soon as I finished the graveside prayers, the bagpiper started playing again. Now the greyhound was really wailing and groaning. It was a sad sight to see the family leaving with Meave, the greyhound, walking away from the grave of its master. The deceased young man's father and mother gave the greyhound tender loving care until it died a few years later.

112

MILKING A COW ON MOUNT TABOR

MOUNT TABOR IS IN GALILEE IN THE HOLY LAND OF ISRAEL. It was on Mount Tabor that Jesus was transfigured in the presence of Peter, James, and John, as recorded in Matthew's Gospel, Chapter 17. Mount Tabor rises from the surrounding flat land in the shape of a large dome. The only way to the top of the mountain is by taxi car. Pilgrims are taken by bus to the base of the mountain. The road to the top of the mountain is very narrow and goes in a zigzag route with several hairpin bends. On the top of the mountain there is the Church of The Transfiguration, where the pilgrims can attend Mass celebrated by the priest, who leads the pilgrimage. There is also a Benedictine Convent and gift shop. The Benedictine Nuns have a few cows grazing there.

I have been to the Holy Land several times. On one of my pilgrimages there, when we reached the top of the mountain, there was a Benedictine Nun milking a cow in a very small field near the church. Having grown up on a dairy farm in Ireland and having milked cows by hand from a young age, I wanted to show off my milking skills to the group traveling with me. I went over to the nun and told her that I was able to milk a cow. I asked her if she would let me milk her cow. She obliged and gave me her milk bucket and stool. I sat down and started milking. My traveling companions were greatly impressed. There was one woman in our group, who was always very nosey and curious. While I was milking, she came closer to me and bent down to get a closer look at my fingers manipulating the cow's teats. When she got close enough to me, I aimed the cow's teat at her face and gave her a squirt of milk between her eyes! She was horrified. Everyone else was amused. Even the little Benedictine Nun was amused. Maybe the cow was also amused! So now I can add it to my resume that I milked a cow on Mount Tabor.

113

THE NORTH AMERICAN COLLEGE

ROME, ITALY

I HAD THE PRIVILEGE TO STUDY AT THE NORTH AMERICAN College in Rome, Italy in 2002, and again in 2014. The North American College is located on the Janiculum Hill and is about a five-minute walk from St. Peter's Basilica. The college is referred to as the NAC. Prior to the year 2000, it took much longer to go from St. Peter's Square to the NAC because one had to walk up the steep Janiculum Hill. For the Jubilee Year of 2000, and to accommodate the many visitors to Rome for that year, a three level parking garage was furrowed out from inside the hill. An escalator was added to each level of the parking garage. This made the distance between St. Peter's and the NAC much shorter.

On both occasions when I lived there, my room window was overlooking the dome of St. Peter's. During my stay there in 2002, John Paul II was pope and living in the papal apartments. I could see his apartment windows from my room. When his lights were out at night, I knew he was in bed! But when I lived there in 2014, Francis had become pope and was not living in the papal apartments.

114

THE ALARM COCK

ROME, ITALY

THE DAY AFTER MY ARRIVAL IN ROME IN 2002, I HAD TO GO shopping for an alarm clock. Because I have a serious hearing loss, I wanted to get a very loud alarm clock. When I found a shop that sold clocks, I went inside. There was a very Italian looking lady behind the counter. I did not speak any Italian, and she did not speak any English. She smiled at me, and she had very long eyelashes. Right away I figured this could be an interesting encounter. When I tried to explain to her in English what I wanted, I was using my hands and pointing to my watch and my ears. She stood there smiling at me and batting her long eyelashes. I pointed to a display of alarm clocks on the shelves behind her. She indicated that she had no idea what I wanted. In frustration, I kept saying to her, "Tick-tock, Tick-tock." I wanted a Tick-Tock and used my arms to demonstrate the big hand and the little hand of a clock in motion. Finally, she figured out what I wanted. She placed a clock on the counter and wound it up. When the alarm went off it did not sound as loud as I wanted. So I had to resort to pointing to my ear and making loud sounds similar to an alarm clock. She brought down another clock, but I was still not satisfied. Within a short time, there were about five different types of alarm clocks on the counter. One of them had two bells and a pecking hen. When she wound up that clock and set off the alarm, it sounded good enough, and I indicated that I would take that one.

But just to be sure that I was satisfied I activated the alarm again. Being pleased with the sound, I turned off the alarm by pressing the stop pin instead of letting it ring out to the end. Now that I was happy with my purchase, the lady put the clock into a box, sealed it with scotch tape, and put it into an attractive shopping bag. When I had paid for the clock, I was able to thank her in Italian. She smiled at me and batted her long eyelashes. I left the shop pleased with myself.

On my way back to the college, I took the three levels of the escalator up through the three levels of the parking garage inside the Janiculum Hill. Going up the second level of the escalator, the alarm clock went off. This happened because I had shut it off in the shop without letting it ring out. When the alarm went off, everyone on the escalator was looking at me. They were probably wondering if I was a terrorist or had a bomb in the bag. I got so flustered that I was unable to open the box, which was sealed with scotch tape. Before I could open the box, the garage security guards had surrounded me on the escalator. They took me aside and checked out the clock and advised me to be more careful in future so as not to cause people to panic thinking, it might be an explosive device on a timer. On my way back to the college, I was thinking, if only the smiling Italian lady with the long eyelashes could see me now!

115

MARIA PISANO
ROME, ITALY

A FEW DAYS LATER, I WENT FOR LUNCH AT A RESTAURANT ON the Via Borgo, which is just outside the walls of Vatican City. Because all the outdoor tables were occupied, I went inside. During my meal, I noticed a woman, who looked elderly carrying a tray loaded with dishes. A younger looking woman was stacking the dishes on to the tray. I considered that the load was getting too heavy for the elderly woman. Suddenly, there was a loud crash of dishes falling on the floor and breaking. The poor old woman looked so embarrassed and got down on her knees to collect the broken pieces and put them back on the tray. My heart ached for her, and I went over to her and got down on my knees to help her. I was dressed as a priest. The old woman was flustered and crying. She indicated that she was very grateful for my help. "Grazie, grazie padre," she cried out and put her hands to my cheeks. Right away I had found a new friend!

As the months went by during my time in Rome, I became a regular customer at that restaurant, and I always went inside to eat. The old woman greeted me with a very affectionate hug and a kiss. We became great friends. One day after lunch, I waited outside for the old woman to get off work. I took her up the street, and we sat at an outdoor table at another restaurant. I did not know any Italian, and she did not know any English. But in spite of this, we had a wonderful conversation! We spoke with our hands. I got her name. Her name was Maria Pisano. She looked very Italian and always wore black clothes. Her face was wrinkled with age, and her hands indicated that she worked very hard during her life. I became a regular customer at her restaurant. I made it a point to go there when it was close to the end of her workday so that I could spend some time with her at an outdoor table. Neither one of us understood what the other was saying, but, somehow we were able to have a wonderful conversation. When the time came for me to leave Rome and return to the United States, our parting was heart-breaking! That year was 2002.

By the year 2005, I was Vicar General for the Diocese of Savannah. That year the Bishop of Savannah was due to travel to Rome for the "Ad Limina" visit with the Pope. Bishops are required to make this visit to the pope every five years to report on the state of the diocese. The Bishop of Savannah at that time was Kevin Boland. As his Vicar General, I travelled to Rome with him. I was far more excited about seeing Maria Pisano again than I was about meeting the Pope!

The very next day after my arrival in Rome with Bishop Boland for the Ad Limina visit with Pope John Paul II, the first item on my agenda was to go and see Maria Pisano at the restaurant. As soon as I arrived, she saw me. She put down her tray, which was loaded as usual with dishes and ran toward me. She hugged me and kissed me and started crying. Mama mia, there we were totally embraced with everyone in the restaurant watching us. I took my seat at a table and watched Maria doing her work with a smile. That was the week before Holy Week. The following Sunday was Palm Sunday. I was scheduled to concelebrate the Mass in St. Peter's Square with the Pope. While eating my lunch, it crossed my mind that Maria, who was born in Rome and lived there all her life, may have never met a pope or even attended a Papal Mass in St. Peter's Square. I decided there and then that I would get Maria a ticket to attend the Papal Mass in St. Peter's Square on Palm Sunday. Not only that, but I would get her a special ticket, which would get her a front row seat very close to the pope. This seat would also enable her to receive Holy Communion from the Pope.

I was very friendly with Monsignor Roger Wroench. He was a classmate of my previous Bishop, who was Bishop Raymond W. Lessard. He was a native of Minnesota, USA, and was based in Rome. He was in charge of providing tickets for papal audiences and special seating for papal Masses for Americans visiting Rome. After my lunch, I went straight to the office of Monsignor Wroench. It was located near the Trevi Fountain. I told him about Maria and my friendship with her. I asked him to provide a ticket for her to attend the papal Mass on Palm Sunday. I insisted that it had to be a special ticket for VIP seating. He was delighted to do this. I went back to the restaurant with the ticket. To make sure that Maria understood what the ticket was for, I got one of the staff in the restaurant, who spoke English and Italian, to act as an interpreter. When I presented Maria with the ticket, she was overcome with emotion. I think she felt like she died and went to heaven! Now I really got plenty of hugging and kissing from her. Through the interpreter, I explained to her that she should meet me at a specified time on Sunday morning at the entrance to St. Peter's Square. I told her that I would hold on to the ticket for her, as I was afraid she might misplace it.

On Palm Sunday morning 2005, I arrived at the entrance to St. Peter's Square dressed in my Monsignor robes, waiting for Maria. Right on time, I could see her walking down the Via della Conciliazione, approaching the entrance to St. Peter's Square. To enter the seating area in the square, we had to go through a security checkpoint. Since Maria never had this experience before, she was somewhat reluctant to go through the scanner. I assured her she would be fine. When we got through security and showed the special VIP ticket to a Swiss Guard, I took Maria up to the very front row of seats right under the papal altar. I could tell that by now Maria was feeling very uneasy in these strange surroundings and would probably prefer to go home. I told her to sit there and say her prayers and wait for the Pope. I had to go and get ready for Mass. I assured her that I would come back to get her after Mass.

During the Mass, I was directly behind the papal altar. I could see Maria in her simple black clothes, sitting there in the middle of others, who considered themselves very important and were dressed in tuxedos and fur coats. Maria sat there among those well-groomed people with her rosary beds in her hands and her lips moving in prayer. When it came time to receive Holy Communion, Maria was escorted by an usher to receive from the Pope. After Mass, I went to her and she had tears running down her cheek. She was very overcome by the experience. I walked back with her to the restaurant and had lunch and watched Maria do what she had been doing every day for many years—collecting dirty dishes on a tray. But this day was different. She began the day by meeting the Pope and receiving Holy Communion from his hand. I met with her employer, who spoke in broken English and thanked him for allowing Maria to have the morning off from work to meet the Pope. He was delighted for her. I bid Maria farewell and told her I would be back the next day to bid her farewell before returning to America for Holy week ceremonies at the Cathedral in Savannah. The following day, we had an emotional parting. The next time I was back in Rome was nine years later in 2014, for more studies at the North American College. By that time, Maria had died and gone to God. May she rest in Peace.

MASS WITH THE POPE

ROME, ITALY

THERE WERE THIRTY-FIVE PRIESTS FROM DIFFERENT DIOCESES in the United States in my class at the North American College in Rome. Two priests from the class concelebrated morning Mass with the Pope in his private chapel. This was done on a rotation bass. On arrival at the Pope's chapel he was in prayer, having been there for a long period before he began Mass. After Mass, he greeted us. The Pope in 2002 was John Paul II. On introducing yourself to the Pope, you stated your name and the name of your diocese. The first time I introduced myself I stated that I was from the Diocese of Savannah in the United States. He looked at me and asked me where I came from before that? When I replied that I came from Tipperary, Ireland, he replied, "It is a long way to Tipperary!"

THE MARTINELLI FAMILY

ROME, ITALY

WHILE AT THE NORTH AMERICAN COLLEGE IN 2002, I WAS introduced to the Martinelli family. Their home was located in the Trastrevere area of Rome. Spanning a few generations of the family, it was a home away from home for foreign priests based in Rome. My introduction to the family came about through two priests in Melbourne, Australia, who were first cousins of my late mother, Bridget Kelly. They were Bishop John Kelly, who was an auxiliary Bishop of Melbourne, and his brother, Father Leo Kelly, who was the Canon Lawyer for the Archdiocese of Melbourne. Their father was John Kelly, who was born in Ireland and was my mother's uncle. He eloped to Australia with a local girl by the name of Foxy Ellie Heffernan when his family did not approve of their plans to get married!

The two Kelly priests from Melbourne had studied in Rome after their ordination. During their years of study in Rome as young foreign priests, the Martinelli home became their home away from home. After their return to Australia, they remained in contact with the Martinelli family. The next generation of the Martinelli family, Salvatore and his wife, Cecilia, continued the practice of extending a welcome to foreign priests based in Rome.

Salvatore and Cecilia Martinelli went on a visit to Australia and spent a few days with Father Leo Kelly in Melbourne. Bishop John Kelly had died some years previously. It so happened that I was also on a visit to Australia at the same time and spent two weeks with Father Leo Kelly. It was at this time that I met Salvatore and Cecilia Martinelli. They assured me that if I was ever in Rome I would be welcome at their home. From this point onward, we corresponded with each other.

Shortly after I arrived in Rome in 2002, I contacted Salvatore and Cecilia Martinelli and they invited me to their home. The details were arranged. When Salvatore arrived at the North American College to collect me, he informed me that he had another priest in the car who was going with us. When I got into the car, Salvatore introduced me to the other priest. This priest was a high profile head of a Vatican department! Mamma mia! I was traveling in style! If my seminary professors could only see me now!

When we arrived at the Martinelli home, there were a few other priests there. We had a very enjoyable meal. This was followed by conversation on a balcony overlooking a piazza below us. When the Vatican official indicated that he was ready to retire for the night, Salvatore Martinelli drove us home. Because the Martinelli home is only about a twenty-minute walk along the banks of the Tiber River, I went there many times. The Martinelli family was willing to collect me and take me home, but I enjoyed the walk along by the Tiber River. Occasionally, when I went to the Martinelli home, that same Vatican official was there. Whenever he was, I did not have to walk home. However, on one occasion, the Vatican official insisted on walking home to his villa. As we walked home together that evening, I again thought of the time in seminary when I sat before a panel of five priests who had to decide if I should be expelled or ordained a priest! Life does take some strange turns! There I was that evening in Rome, walking along with a Vatican official by the banks of the Tiber River, telling him stories! He was enjoying them. I mentioned to him that people were encouraging me to put my stories in writing. He endorsed the suggestion! I told him that I would include him in my stories. He gave his consent, but asked me not to mention his name because he preferred to keep his social life private.

118

ANGELINA, THE BEGGAR WOMAN

ROME, ITALY

In 2014, I returned to Rome for more study at the North American Colleges. By this time Pope Benedict had resigned and Francis was pope. My friend Maria Pisano was dead, but I formed a friendship with another elderly Italian woman by the name of Angelina. Angelina was one of the many beggar women in St. Peter's Square. She was badly stooped over and had one tooth in front of her mouth. She was leaning on a walking stick in her right hand and holding out her left hand with a tin can for collecting coins. She had an old tattered satchel hanging from her shoulder. It probably contained all of her earthly possessions. There are plenty of beggar women in St. Peter's Square, but somehow Angelina became my favorite. I could never pass her without placing a few coins in her tin can. There was something about her pitiful looking face and badly stooped body that touched my heart. Hardly a day went by that I was not in St. Peter's Square. Whenever Angelina saw me coming, the pitiful look on her face became more pitiful! She held out her tin can and from her stooped body she would cry out. "Grazie padre!" My heart would be moved at seeing her.

During Holy Week of that year, I participated in all the ceremonies in St. Peter's Basilica with Pope Francis. On the Holy Thursday, morning I concelebrated the Mass of Chrism. On the way out from the Basilica after Mass, I saw Angelina in her usual begging posture. I was dressed in my Monsignor robes. St. Peter's Square was thronged with visitors. I wanted Angelina to do well that day because of the large crowd of visitors. I walked up to her and put a few coins in her tin can. Tourists who looked very affluent were walking past Angelina and ignoring her. I was getting the urge to rob them! I thought of a way that would attract their attention to Angelina. I stood next to her in all my Monsignor regalia and put my left arm around her shoulder and pointed toward her with my right hand. Looking pitifully at those who walked by Angelina, I kept repeating over and over again in my best Italian, "*Questa e mia sorella maggiore.*" Translated to English it is, "*This is my older sister.*" This certainly got the attention of the tourists. They were looking at me in amazement and then looked with pity at Angelina! Now they started putting coins in her tin can. It soon filled up. She needed a larger tin can! Angelina had to unload the tin can full of coins into her satchel. I was getting worried in case the Vatican Police noticed this and arrested Angelina and myself for robbing the tourists. I decided that enough was enough, and it was time to go. I bid Angelina farewell and got lost in the crowd and went back to the college. Next day, Good Friday, I met Angelina with her walking stick and tin can and satchel. I was worried about where she might have hidden the money from the previous day because she was homeless. I had a suspicion it was in her satchel. A few days later when it was time for me to return to the United States, I bid Angelina a tearful farewell there in St. Peter's Square and gave her some Euro notes to deposit into her satchel. I have not been back to Rome since 2014, and I have no idea what became of Angelina. Blessed are the poor in spirit. Someday I hope to return to the Eternal City. It keeps calling me back!

119

MY VISIT TO SOUTH KOREA

IN 2009, I SPENT A FEW WEEKS IN SOUTH KOREA AND China. I always wanted to travel to the Orient. In South Korea, I stayed with Father Noel O'Neill, who is a Columban Missionary priest. In a previous story about my studies for the priesthood, I mentioned my interest in the Columban Missions. My time in South Korea was delightful. In time, I got used to removing my shoes upon entering a house. The one thing I could not manage was sitting on the floor, or squatting on the floor, as is the custom there.

One weekend, Father Noel took me to a Buddhist Monastery where we stayed overnight. We joined the monks in prayer. We dressed in an orange color uniform and slept on the floor. During the night, we had to get up and go to prayer with the monks. All the monks were squatted on the floor and meditating. Because I was unable to squat, I sat down on the floor with my back propped up to a wall and with my legs stretched out. I was comfortable in this position. After the prayer session was over, I returned to my sleeping quarters with Father Noel.

He informed me that the monks were watching me and probably tolerating my unorthodox posture. But he also told me that there was a young monk looking very annoyed at me. It seems that the young monk made attempts to go to me and reprimand me, but an older monk stopped him.

On another occasion, we went to eat at a restaurant with a group of young people. The table was about one foot off the ground. Everyone was squatting on the floor at the table. Since I was unable to squat, I had to sit on my bottom with my legs stretched out under the table. My back was killing me, and I was so glad when the meal was over.

Whenever Father Noel celebrated Mass, the altar was a little table about one foot off the floor. He celebrated Mass squatting at the altar. I was concelebrating Mass with him, but I had to sit on a chair next to him.

Other than my problem with squatting on the floor, I really enjoyed my time in South Korea. The people were extremely friendly. Even at the toll stations on the motorways, the person collecting the toll from the driver of a car engaged in friendly conversation. What impressed me most was the vast number of people, who attended church and their prayerfulness.

After some time in South Korea, I went to China. On my return from China, I spent some more time in South Korea. During this time, another Columban priest took me to the North Korean border. As we drove along the highway, the closer we got to the border, the traffic became less and less. By the time we reached the border, we were the only car on the road. It was an eerie feeling looking at the lookout posts along the way. When we got to the border, we had to stop at barricades, which were several hundred yards away from the border checkpoint. We got out of the car for a look. While we were there a flock of geese flew over the border from South Korea into North Korea. I remarked that the geese had freedom of travel or movement and were not restricted by any territorial borders. In spite of the spooky and eerie feeling, I said to the other priest that I would wave my hand toward the border to send greetings to North Korea. He growled at me not to dare do that so as not to attract the attention of the guards at the checkpoint. But being hardheaded, I did it anyway. At that very moment, a convoy of military trucks came driving toward us from the checkpoint. Dear Lord, I thought they are coming to get me, and I will be taken as a prisoner into North Korea. My heart was pounding. When they got to the barricades where we were standing, the convoy turned around and headed back. It turned out that they were coming to escort a few cars into North Korea. I was relieved, and my priest friend decided it was time to go before I caused trouble. A few days later I returned to America stopping off in Tokyo, Japan.

120

THE CHINESE STREET GIRL

WHILE IN SOUTH KOREA, I MADE A TRIP TO CHINA. I SPENT about a week in Beijing. This was a wonderful experience. The architecture is fascinating. Everything there is so colorful. I enjoyed visiting such places as The Forbidden City, The Great Wall of China, and the 2008 Olympic Grounds, and Tiananmen Square. Before going to China, I was warned that the girls on the street like to walk with Western people to practice their English.

One day while walking along a street footpath admiring the architecture, a young Chinese girl approached me and in very broken English asked me if she could walk with me to practice her English. Being an adventurous person, I thought this could be an interesting experience for me. I agreed to have her walk with me. She immediately put her arm into my arm. We walked along, and she did most of the talking. I was paying very little attention to her because I did not understand what she was saying, and I was admiring the architecture. Occasionally, I would just respond by saying, "Yes, yes." Because I had a slight suspicion that this girl might be a "hooker," I thought I should be more careful about saying, "Yes, Yes." That could lead to an unplanned adventure. So I began to pay more attention to what she was saying. I kept responding, "I do not know." Since she did not seem to understand my Tipperary accent, I began to speak in broken English imitating her accent as best I could. We walked along for a few blocks. By now, I was wondering how I was going to get rid of her. Otherwise, I thought I might be taking her home to my Bishop!

We arrived at a traffic light and stopped for the light to change before we could cross the street. While standing at the light, the street girl said to me, "Me and you doing very good. Me like to take you to get coffee." Right away I suspected that she had more than coffee on her mind! I thought to myself that I must get rid of her right now. A great idea crossed my mind. I decided to tell her that I was going to meet a friend, who was a policeman. If she was a hooker, she would vanish immediately. So in my best broken English and Chinese accent, I said, "Me and you doing good. But me meet friend who is a policeman. He waiting for me at next light." As soon as I said this, she said, "Me forget. Me must be go now." Then she ran off like a rabbit. I walked on ready to meet another Chinese hooker. I could use the policeman story again!

Shortly after that, I came upon a place where bicycles were rented out. Since there were plenty of people in China riding bicycles, I decided to rent one. By doing this, I could cycle around Beijing and see the sights and avoid the street girls. I cycled for about an hour and returned the bicycle. Then I took one of those three wheel motor taxi bikes back to my hotel. Some days later, I returned to South Korea without a Chinese street girl to introduce to my Bishop!

121

A RUSSIAN LADY NAMED OLGA

After I retired in 2013, I became a member of The Apostleship of the Sea. This enables me to serve as a chaplain on Holland-America cruise ships. It gives me the opportunity to visit places I could only dream of. Being a chaplain on cruise ships can be a very enjoyable experience. There is daily Mass celebrated in a theatre, as well as Sunday Mass. As a Catholic chaplain, I can conduct Sunday services for passengers, who are Protestant. Some passengers are anxious to talk with the chaplain about personal matters. It might be the recent death of a spouse, a troubled marriage, or some other personal matter. I could write several stories about some of my experiences as a chaplain on the cruise ships I served on.

My most memorable cruise was a two-week cruise on the Baltic Sea. The ship left from Rotterdam in Holland. We stopped at Denmark, Estonia, Germany, Russia, Finland, Sweden, Denmark again, and ending up back at Rotterdam. Stopping at the above named places, sightseeing tours were available. Before arriving at a port, passengers could sign up in advance for their choice of tour from a brochure provided. We spent two days docked at Saint Petersburg in Russia. To enter Russia, one must have a visa. For tourists, a group visa will suffice. Later in this story, I will relate a serious problem I had with the group visa because I did not stay with the group. I was lucky I was not arrested and sent to Siberia! More on this toward the end of the story.

Before arriving in St Petersburg, I signed up for a Panoramic Tour of the city. On arrival and before disembarking the ship, I collected my boarding pass to get on the tour bus. The bus number was 22. Greeting us at the entrance to the bus, was our very attractive young lady who was going to be our tour guide. After everyone was seated on the bus, the tour guide boarded. She welcomed us on board and told us that her name was Olga. She spoke perfect English. As we drove around, Olga went into great detail pointing out the various places of interest. She also gave us a history lesson on the period of the czars, the revolution, and the era of the Soviet Union.

Along the way we stopped at various places for a walking tour. We also stopped at a few gift shops. At one of those stops, I did not go inside. Instead, I had a most enjoyable chat sitting on an outdoor bench seat with Olga. From that time onward, we had several chats while others went into gift shops. On the first day, we stopped for lunch on our own. Olga suggested some restaurants or cafes nearby. I found a pub where I got a steak and kidney pie along with a pint of Russian ale. The inside of the pub was dark and dingy and was very similar to an old-time Irish pub. After I had my meal, I went outside and sat on a bench seat and watched the people go by. At this time, I had about thirty minutes to spare until I was due back at the bus. While I was sitting there, Olga came along by herself. We walked back toward the bus. On the way, she took me to see the inside of the Church of the Spilled Blood where one of the czars was murdered. Hence the name 'spilled blood.' This church was used as a warehouse during the Soviet era and is now a museum. After this, we got on the bus for some more sightseeing and returned to the ship in time for our evening meal. After our meal, we assembled again for a guided tour of the Hermitage Museum, which was formerly the palace of the czars.

Next day, we had another guided tour of the city on bus number 22 with Olga as our tour guide. Again, there was time to get lunch on our own. By now Olga had noticed that I was traveling alone. She offered to take me to lunch. During lunch, I found out from Olga that she was married and that her husband was a police officer. She knew that I was the chaplain on the cruise ship and told me that she was a member of the Russian Orthodox Church. This led to a discussion on the relationship between the Russian Orthodox Church and the Roman Catholic Church. After lunch, we returned to the bus for some more sightseeing. At the end of the tour of the city, we returned to the ship around six o'clock in the evening. The cruise ship was not leaving until nine o'clock. It was going to Helsinki, Finland. Having three hours to spare, and instead of having my evening meal on the ship, I asked Olga if I could take her to dinner. Without hesitation, she was delighted to accept my offer.

We got into her car and she drove to a restaurant, which was some distance from where the ships were docked. We had a very enjoyable meal and because her English was so perfect it was a pleasure chatting with her. She asked me some questions about Ireland and talked about life in Russia after the collapse of the Soviet Union. I was surprised to find out from her that many people in Russia preferred the way of life during the Soviet era. The State took care of their basic needs. Now they found it difficult to survive. However, they did appreciate their new freedom. My time with Olga during this meal went by very fast. When I looked at my watch, I got a shock when I saw that I had only about thirty minutes to get back to the ship before it left for Finland. Olga drove at great speed back to the ship. I was worried in case she might get stopped for speeding and then I would be delayed and the ship would leave without me.

When we arrived back at the ship with very little time to spare, my group visa became an issue. Thinking that there might be a problem at the immigration checkpoint because I did not have a visa, I asked Olga to stay with me to make sure that I got clearance. She said that if the immigration officer insisted on my having a visa she would make up a story. She would tell him that she took me on a private tour away from the group. On entering the immigration control area, the place was almost in darkness. There was only one desk open, and there was an older man sitting there reading a paper. I presented all my travel documents as well as my chaplain card. The old man carefully checked everything. Then he asked the dreaded question! He asked me for my visa! I explained that I had a group visa. His English was very broken. He asked, "Where is group? Me see no group here." Holding up his fingers he pointed to them saying, "Group is this, this, this and more this." I replied, in broken English, which I thought would help him better understand. I replied, "Group is on ship." Then he said, "Why you not on ship?" I tried to explain that I ran late and was with lady over there as I pointed toward Olga. I motioned to Olga to come over to help me. When she came over, I said to the old man, "Now we have group, two people." With this he got mad at me and slammed the desk saying, "You not understand. Group is much people." By now, I thought, will I be arrested and sent to Siberia? Olga then tried to explain things to him. She was speaking in Russian, so I do not know what she told him. Whatever she said worked, but he did not appear to be happy with her. He stamped my papers with such force that I though the desk would break. Then he threw the documents at me and raised both hands in the air screaming something in Russian. Olga looked at me, and said she was sorry that the old man had to be so difficult. We hugged each other and went our separate ways.

The horn on the ship was now blaring to signal departure time. When I got out to where the ships were docked, there were four ships lined up behind each other, and my ship was the last one. I hurried toward the gangway. When I got to the top of the gangway, it was pulled up behind me, and one of the crew members, who was from Vietnam, recognized me as being the chaplain, said, "Fadda, Fadda, you almost miss ship." During the remainder of the cruise, I stayed with the group when on shore.

122

AN OBESE WOMAN ON A CRUISE SHIP

THERE CAN BE HUMOROUS HAPPENINGS ON BOARD A CRUISE ship. On one particular cruise there was a very obese woman. She was a good sport and was very aware of the fact that everyone took notice of her size. I think she deliberately attracted attention and made fun of herself making humorous comments about her overweight. The following is an example of this.

The ship had fourteen levels of floors. There were several elevators located throughout the ship. It was a sight to watch the obese woman get on an elevator. She had a very large chest matched with a corresponding very large posterior. She was equally large in width. Her hands could not hang straight from her shoulders. They were always extended outward like wings. Getting on an elevator, she had to go on it alone. There was no way that anyone could fit in with her.

On entering an elevator, she got her chest in first facing forward. Then she had to bring her rear end after her. Because her rear end was so large it was sticking out, and the elevator door could not close. Because her two hands were sticking out like wings, she had to raise them above her head. When she finally got herself into the elevator, she had to wiggle around so that she was sideways in the elevator with her chest pressed tightly against the wall in front of her and her rear end pressed tightly against the wall behind her. She was really and truly wall to wall. Because her hand next to the elevator door was sticking out again, the elevator door could not close. She solved the problem by raising both arms over her head. Now she was unable to push the button for the floor of her destination. One of her friends with her had to stick their hand into the elevator to push the button and quickly withdraw it to allow the door to close. Then she was on her way up or down to the cheers of the onlookers. Another friend was waiting at the door of her arrival. When she arrived and the door opened, that friend who was waiting for her had to hold the door open. The obese woman now had to wiggle around again so as to get her rear end facing the elevator door and reverse out. Passengers waiting at the door cheered as she emerged. She seemed to enjoy all this attention by making humorous comments about her size. The poor woman was so big that no chair could seat her. A special seat was provided for her in the dining room where she took up the entire side of a table. She was a good sport!

123

IRISH-AMERICAN VOCABULARY

DURING MY FIRST YEAR IN AMERICA, I DISCOVERED THAT
even though we all spoke English, that words often had
different meanings. The following are some examples:

A homely woman. In Ireland, it is complimentary to refer to
a woman as being homely. But in America the word homely
means not attractive. In my first year in America, when invited
to the home of a parishioner for dinner, I frequently complimented the lady of the house by telling her that she was very
homely. I had no idea that what I thought was a compliment
was in fact an insult. It was only after I had done this a few
times that I learned about my mistake.

Fag. In Ireland a fag is a cigarette. I was a heavy smoker. When
teaching in school on the day before Ash Wednesday, I was
encouraging the children to give up something for Lent. When

they asked me what I was giving up I innocently told them I was giving up fags, and since I was very fond of fags, I was going to miss them very much. That night the pastor came to my room very upset. He told me that he was getting phone calls from parents, who were upset because I told the children in school that I was giving up fags for Lent and that I would miss them very much. The Pastor had to explain to me the American meaning of the word and cautioned me never to use it again!

Craic. This word is pronounced as "Crack." It is the Gaelic word for fun. People in Ireland frequently say things such as— the craic in the pub last night was great! Or something like— there is always great craic in such and such a place.

124

RETIREMENT

IN 2013, I RELUCTANTLY RETRIED BECAUSE OF HEALTH ISSUES. This was a major shock to my system. I missed the challenges of parish administration and being in charge! It took me about two years to adjust to this new lifestyle. I opted to continue living at the Cathedral Rectory where I had lived for the previous seventeen years. I did not want to live elsewhere in an apartment because this would remove me completely from any parish involvement. I have always liked to live over the store. The big disadvantage in staying on at the Cathedral was not being in charge and watching my successor doing things his way. But I was grateful that he allowed me to continue living there. I promised not to interfere in any way in his administration or decisions he made. Retired priests who continue to live in the Parish House are required to pay a monthly rent for their room and board. The amount of rent is the equivalent of the rental of an apartment. The advantage is that meals and laundry are included. This may come as a surprise to many who think that retired priests have free lodging! It is understood that the retired priest in residence helps with the celebration of Masses and other sacramental duties.

Because I am a 'people person,' I never meet a stranger. I like to meet people and chat with them. As mentioned elsewhere in this collection of stories, Savannah is the sixth most visited city in the United States. Tourists flock to Savannah. They can take guided city tours on trolleys, horse-drawn carriages, or pedicabs. The Cathedral is one of the stopping points on the tours. Because of this, several hundred people visit the Cathedral each day and are given guided tours. Frequently, I walk out into the Cathedral during the day dressed as a priest and mingle with the tourists. I meet some of the most interesting people from various parts of the world. Some of them have never met a priest before. Occasionally, I will meet someone who is very troubled, and this gives me the opportunity to continue an active priestly ministry.

For a few years after retiring, I made regular visits to the three local hospitals and the many nursing homes where we have parishioners. At one time, I made monthly house calls to twenty-six elderly parishioners. Elsewhere in this collection are two stories about home visits. One is the story about going in the window of a house and meeting two policemen on my way out. The other story is about the bed of the old woman collapsing.

At the Cathedral in Savannah on June 4, 2017, I celebrated the Golden Jubilee of my ordination. A very large number of parishioners attended. My sister and her husband travelled from Ireland. Relatives from New York and friends from various parts of the United States were present, as well as parishioners from parishes where I previously served. Bishop Gregory Hart-mayer, the Bishop of Savannah, and Bishop Kevin Boland, the retired Bishop of Savannah, and several priests were also present. There were also people from other local religious denominations present as well as their ministers. I have always maintained a close relationship with the local ministers of other faiths. The attendance also included friends who are Jewish, Moslem, Hindu, and Buddhist, and, last but not least, friends who never attend church.

At my home parish of St. Nicholas in Solohead, near Tipperary, Ireland, on August 10, 2017, I celebrated my Golden Jubilee. Attending were family members, relatives, friends, and parishioners. Also attending, were classmates from Wexford, clergy from the local Archdiocese of Cashel and Emly, and other priest friends. The homily was given by Bishop Denis Brennan, Bishop of Ferns, who was with me in seminary in Wexford. There was also a large gathering present from County Wexford, whom I got to know during my years in Wexford. Last but not least, two parishioners from the Cathedral in Savannah, Melanie Brooks and Maria Finn, traveled all the way from the United States for the occasion. The attendance there was similar in size to the attendance at my First Mass some fifty years earlier. The big difference was that most of the people who attended my First Mass were gone to God and were replaced by others, who were not born at that time.

Even though I am now retired with some health issues, I hope to continue in some form of priestly ministry for whatever length of time the Good Lord allows me to have in this world. I have many happy memories and hope to accumulate more as time goes on. I mentioned in my introduction that some of the stories I have written in this collection may appear as outlandish! Take my word, they are all true! They were what they were. They are what they are. They will be what they will be.

ACKNOWLEDGMENTS

I would like to acknowledge my sister, Nuala. She and I are the only surviving members of our immediate family. Brothers PJ, Michael, and Owen Roe have joined our parents in the here-after. Family is very important to me, and I am grateful for the values imparted to me as the oldest son of this family. Nuala was only a child when I left Ireland for America, yet now she has become the anchor to my Irish heritage.

I have been encouraged in my vocation by many teachers, professors, bishops, and fellow priests, some of whom have made it into the pages of this collection. I value their contributions to my life.

I also have friends and families on both sides of the Atlantic, who have been frequent listeners of these stories and whose reactions prompted me to collect them into this book.

I would also like to thank close friends, Melanie Brooks,

Glenda Sanders, Stephen Williams, and Father Thomas Peyton for their assistance getting to publication. Any grammar issues or sentences that go on far too long are intentional. The structures of these stories are in keeping with a rural Irish dialect and are part of my story-telling techniques. We have elected to leave these as is so the voice you hear in these pages is uniquely my own.

Thanks to the artistic abilities of Fiona Jayde for the wonderful cover design.

I would also like to thank Emily Heid and Bootstrap Books for her assistance in shepherding this manuscript through the publication process and teaching this old dog new tricks. If you ever need help with publishing, Emily is the one to contact.

And lastly, thanks to you who thought this little book was worth your investment of time and money. God's blessing on you.

Monsignor William Oliver O'Neill

ABOUT THE AUTHOR

Born in 1942 in County Tipperary, Ireland, and educated at Irish schools and seminary, William Oliver O'Neill accepted the call to "mission" work in the American rural south. He left home and family at the age of 25 and crossed the ocean to a world of new family, new friends, and very different ideas of life. Many Europeans, who immigrated to America never returned to their native land, but O'Neill was determined that he would remain Irish at heart and has returned home at least once a year for the last 53 years. He served parishes in New Orleans, Augusta, Georgia, and Columbus, Georgia, before ending up in Savannah where he spent the last 32 years of his pastoral career serving in two of the city's larger parishes. He attended the North American College in Rome on two occasions to extend his education and has traveled to many countries outside of his native Ireland and adopted America. He is known for his amazing memory and the stories he can pull up for any occasion.